Gratitude doesn't lead to happiness.

Gratitude *is* happiness

In its most obtainable form.

Published by Familius™ LLC, www.familius.com

Familius books are available at special discounts for bulk purchases for sales promotions, family or corporate use. Special editions, including personalized covers, excerpts of existing books, or books with corporate logos, can be created in large quantities for special needs. For more information, contact Premium Sales at 559-876-2170 or email specialmarkets@familius.com.

Library of Congress Catalog-in-Publication Data

2014943625

pISBN 978-1939629401

Edited by Amy Stewart
Cover and book design by David Miles

10 9 8 7 6 5 4 3 2 1

First Edition

FAMILIUS

RICHARD AND LINDA EYRE

THE THANKFUL HEART

HOW DELIBERATE GRATITUDE CAN
CHANGE EVERY TEXTURE OF OUR LIVES

This little book is intimate,
Because it follows the journey of one family
into and through gratitude.

This big book is vast,
Because it embraces appreciation for the entire universe.

And we, ourselves, are so small that we can slip from a landscape,
But so large that we can hold the sun.

This is a book about finding beauty in the tiniest hint of a smile,
Or the most magnificent, sweeping horizon.

But it is mostly about locating our own hearts,
By following the map we call Thanks-Giving.

CONTENTS

It is no bland or passive quality we are talking about here.
Thanksgiving is not just a second-tier holiday,
And Thanks-Giving is not just a nice, polite thing to do.

We are talking about something much more than that—
About a holiday that can become the harbinger
Of a Grace-filled Christmas and a Joy-filled New Year,

And we are talking
About an obtainable skill that can transform your life,
About a habit that can reframe your perspective and your outlook,
About an extraordinary gift you can receive from God
And give to others,
About a secret that can unlock the deepest and most beautiful
Parts of your heart.

PART ONE

THE SECRETS OF THANKS-GIVING

A TRADITION, A SKILL, A GIFT, AND A CONNECTION TO JOY

Making Thanksgiving the Harbinger of Our Holidays . . . and then Extending and Expanding It Through the Rest of the Year

Harbinger: "Something that prepares, provides, presages, or foreshadows what is to come." This is exactly what Thanksgiving can do for Christmas and for the whole new year that follows.

This is a book about practicing gratitude (and getting better at it) year-round, not just on the fourth Thursday in November. Still, what a good thing it is that we have a holiday once a year to remind us. So let's begin with that holiday . . .

Thanksgiving Traditions

It's interesting how traditions begin. Years ago, for our growing family, the Thanksgiving weekend was a time for scrambling around, seeing grandparents and trying to get started on some Christmas shopping. Thanksgiving Day itself was all about the food and the football. Our Thanksgiving traditions were to eat way too much and to watch the Macy's parade in the morning and as many

games as we could find all afternoon and evening. It was nice because everyone was together, but other than the blessing on the food, our day had very little to do with Thanks or with Giving or with anything connected to gratitude.

Then one year, something happened quite by chance. The parade was getting a little long, the turkey had another couple of hours to cook, and the kids were a bit bored. Wanting to make something happen, I grabbed a roll of calculator paper—that tells you how long ago it was—and yelled, "Hey, let's play a game while we wait for dinner." The game was making a list of everything we could think of that we were thankful for.

What made it work was that we have a bunch of competitive kids. They each got caught up in putting more things on the list than anyone else. Someone would yell something out, and I would write it down and number it on the narrow, unrolling paper. I would yell out, "Forty . . . fifty!" as the list grew.

The first few things on the list were obvious—"freedom," "parents," "shoes,"—but as we went over one hundred, some of them got a little obscure—"doorknobs," "potato peelers." I would say something like, "Come on, are you really thankful for that?" and the kid would say, "Sure, how would we open doors?"

That first year, we got to five hundred. (That number became our goal at about four hundred, when someone said, "Let's keep going, we are almost to five hundred.") We strung the list up like crepe paper above the dining table, and the spirit and conversation of gratitude held up throughout the meal. A tradition was born.

The next Thanksgiving, of course, we had to break our record and we got to six hundred.

We kept all those rolls of paper— all those lists of gratitude—each a testament to the blessings and the joys of a year almost past.

As our children got older, and as Thanksgivings were spent with extended families and friends, the thankful list evolved into a thankful game: Each person makes a list of ten unique things he is profoundly grateful for, and then each list is read out loud. Any blessing that is also on someone else's list has to be crossed off so that each person's score is the number of things listed that no one else thought of.

Well before either the "Thankful List" or the "Thankful Game," the two of us had decided to send out Thanksgiving cards rather than Christmas cards. Part of our reasoning was a bit selfish—we figured that everyone who received a Thanksgiving card from us would be reminded to send us a Christmas card, which would brighten up the rest of our holidays.

And with that decision, we began a tradition that has now lasted for more than forty years. Each year as the days shorten and the leaves change from green to brilliant red and gold, we try to refocus our thanks-giving and to construct some kind of a poem or greeting that both gives and expresses gratitude, and that perhaps reflects some new perspective on the art and the joy and the practice of genuine thankfulness. The backlighting of gratitude puts our everyday lives into sharp relief, and we feel more and love more.

In this book's concluding section, we include these forty-three poems—which you will see progress from what may be overly simple to what may be overly complex—to share our own

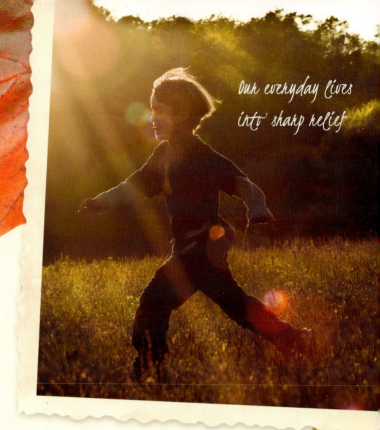

Our everyday lives into sharp relief

evolving thought on Thanks-Giving and what it can mean in our lives.

The Perfect Timing of Thanksgiving

Thanksgiving is the holiday of peace, the celebration of work and the simple life. . . . a true folk-festival that speaks the poetry of the turn of the seasons, the beauty of seedtime and harvest, the ripe product of the year, and the deep, deep connection of all these things with God.

RAY STANNARD BAKER

This book was written exactly 150 years after President Abraham Lincoln established an annual, national observance of "Thanksgiving and Praise to our beneficent Father who dwelleth in the Heavens." In that beautiful proclamation, he said, "The year that is drawing towards its close, has been filled with the blessings of fruitful fields and healthful skies."

Being thankful has always been viewed as an attribute and a gift—and one that is connected to happiness, to health, and to harmony.

The Thanksgiving holiday reminds us each year of what we have to be thankful for—but also of our need to increase our gratitude, and to extend and expand it throughout the year.

The Perfect Sequence of Our Holidays

Have you ever thought about the interesting sequence of our four year-ending holidays?

Packed into the final sixth of the year, we have Halloween, then Thanksgiving, then Christmas and Hanukkah, and then New Year's Eve.

As each year begins to wind down, we enter winter via a strange holiday that celebrates fear and ghoulishness and allows us to escape ourselves with masks and costumes. Next we get the sweet pause of a long football and feasting weekend to remember our heritage and our blessings. Then, if we can lift above the commercialization of it all, we honour the birth of Christ and the peace and goodwill of men. Finally, we party out the old year and make resolutions for the new.

Another way to conceptualize this sequence is that Thanksgiving lifts us from Halloween to Christmas—that gratitude and acknowledgement of God pull us from hell to heaven and set us up to look optimistically and spiritually toward the new year.

We love to view Thanksgiving as the transition, the transformer, and the transfer from the stress and exhaustion of the first eleven months and from the darkness of Halloween to the peace and light of Christmas and the fresh start of another year.

The Perfect Time of Year

Especially for those who live in four-season climates, Thanksgiving is wonderfully placed. As late autumn begins to yield to winter, it seems to set the stage for a more reflective outlook and for mentally inventorying our blessings and setting them up as a bulwark against the coming snow and cold. Like walking through dry, fragrant piles of fallen autumn leaves, we can rustle our souls and summon a greater awareness of beauty and a healthier perspective that connects past and future blessings.

But sadly, in our broader society, Thanksgiving is the holiday that is getting lost. It is becoming marginalized into a convenient long weekend that gives us a head start on our holiday shopping. Turkeys and Pilgrims don't even see the light of day as merchandisers pull down the witches and monsters on the same morning that they put up Santa and the trees and stockings. Popular culture shifts seamlessly from devils to divinity without even a pause for reflection and receiving.

But, as Barbara Rainey put it,

> Thanksgiving remains the holiday of "coming home." It's a holiday of rest—in stark contrast to the frenzy of obligation and spending that threatens to destroy the essence of Christmas. . . . It is . . . a holiday for celebrating faith, family, and freedom.

No Americans have been more impoverished than these who, nevertheless, set aside a day of thanksgiving.

Today, despite blessings beyond what the Pilgrims could imagine, we are losing the vital, life-sustaining emotion of gratitude. Our tendency to take things for granted is shocking.

We often take for granted the very things that most deserve our gratitude.

CYNTHIA OZICK

As the Thanksgiving holiday itself is being obliterated—squeezed down to nothing by the ghouls of Halloween on one side and the ever-earlier commercial interest of Christmas on the other—we each need to make a personal commitment to gratitude.

While Christians originated the holiday, no one group of Christians or non-Christians have eminent domain on Thanksgiving. Ponder the similar sentiments of the scriptures of sundry faiths:

To have gratitude . . . can help us soften and open to feelings of expansiveness and connection.

DHAMMAPADA (BUDDHIST)

Let us come before His presence with thanksgiving, and make a joyful noise.

OLD TESTAMENT, PSALMS 95:2

Live in thanksgiving daily. . . .When thou risest in the morning let thy heart be full of thanks to God.

BOOK OF MORMON, ALMA 34:38, 37:37

Any who is grateful does so to the profit of his own soul.

QUR'AN 031.012

The lofty goals of this little book, at least with you, its readers, are to return Thanksgiving to the forefront; to make it the harbinger of the holidays and the perfect preparation for Christmas; to change our personal spelling and meaning to "Thanks-Giving;" to make the whole concept into a major heartfelt verb instead of a minor holiday noun, and then to run it up on the beach of the whole coming year.

In Tribute to Thanksgiving

Thanksgiving has been called the American Holiday. It was born out of gratitude in times of deep adversity but boundless opportunity.

The hardships of the hardy souls we call Pilgrims were almost unimaginable, yet the boundless thanks they felt for their newfound freedom and the opportunity and options of a new land—along with the gratitude for having made it across the ocean—prompted them to set aside a special day of Thanksgiving.

H. U. Westermayer used these Pilgrims to remind us that gratitude is a choice we can make no matter what:

The Pilgrims made seven times more graves than huts.

He who receiveth all things with thankfulness shall be made glorious.

DOCTRINE AND COVENANTS 78:19

I, remembering Thee with grateful spirit, a mortal, call with might on thee immortal.

RIG VEDA (SANSCRIT HINDU) BK5.4.VS9

Thanksgiving bridges differences and puts all humans onto a humble, happy plane where we focus on what we have rather than what we lack.

Elevating from Thanksgiving to Thanks-Giving

Thanksgiving, after all, is a word of action.

W. J. CAMERON

Besides being a verb, Thanks-Giving can also be a somewhat divine adjective, as in "a thanks-giving heart."

When we make thanks-giving a verb we have something to apply, something to practice, something to give back, and we move mentally into new plateaus of adventure. And when we make it an adjective, it works to enhance all of our most important parts . . . a thankful heart, a grateful mind, an appreciative life.

Instead of using Thanksgiving to eat turkey, we can use it to awaken our awareness, to prick our perspective, to lengthen our love, and to connect our spirits to God.

Instead of letting it lie like an offering on an altar, we can exercise it like a muscle, strap it on our backs like a pack, and aim it like a ray at the recognized source of all blessings.

Grasping the Greatness of Gratitude

God gave you a gift of 86,400 seconds today. Have you used one to say "thank you?"

WILLIAM A. WARD

Is there one single quality, or attribute, or sentiment that could legitimately be called

- The easiest gift to give

- The noblest of virtues

- The bringer or precipitator of other virtues and the antidote to evil

- In fact the very definition of virtues

- Even the parent of all other virtues

- The highest form of thought

- The multiplier of happiness

- The biggest difference-maker among virtuous and non-virtuous people

Move into new plateaus of adventure

The Secret

There is a secret key to happiness—even to joy—that is available to all but used by few.

It is one of those things that is hidden in plain sight—something that we know intuitively and yet do not focus on as much as we should. It is the fact that gratitude precipitates joy. In fact, gratitude is a form of joy, and joy is a form of gratitude.

Studies reveal that feelings of gratitude trigger oxytocin, the chemical that makes your brain feel happiness. And while there are no studies for it, we know from experience that feelings of gratitude also trigger a closer connection with the Spirit of God, which makes your soul feel happiness.

Besides being a secret, it is a consistent, reliable, and proportionate mathematical formula: $<G = <J$ (more gratitude equals more joy)

Note that joy and happiness, while related, are not the same thing. An anonymous poet may have said it best:

> Happiness is a thing of here and now,
>
> The bright leaf in the hand, the moment's sun,
>
> The fight accomplished or the summit won.

> Happiness is a lifting, buoyant kind of thing,
>
> That lifts the bird more surely on its wing.
>
> When things go well, happiness may start,
>
> But Joy is secret smiling of the heart.

Joy can coexist with sorrow and even with pain. Fear and joy can bounce off of each other.

Joy is the positive interpretation of all mortal experience, and thus the purpose of life.

The magic of the secret is that gratitude is the most obtainable kind of joy. Because unlike happiness, gratitude can actually be practiced—it is a skill that can be developed and a habit that can be learned. And gratitude attracts joy always, not only to its practicer but also to its recipient.

When directed to God, a consistent and constant attitude of gratitude acknowledges His divine hand in every aspect of our lives. It ensures humility. It awakens wonder. It prompts perception and perspective. It bequeaths empathy. It opens visions. It expresses love. It warms hearts.

> I WOULD MAINTAIN THAT THANKS ARE THE HIGHEST FORM OF THOUGHT; AND THAT GRATITUDE IS HAPPINESS DOUBLED BY WONDER.
>
> —G.K. CHESTERTON

Gratitude awakens wonder.

It prompts perception and perspective.

It bequeaths empathy.

It opens visions.

It expresses love.

It warms hearts.

We struggle with these questions until we realize with our real eyes that there is one last thing to be grateful for—and it is the gift of gratitude itself. On some levels, thanksgiving is something we summon or build up in and for ourselves. But the deepest gratitude is a gift of the Spirit. Like all of God's gifts, this higher form is not something we earn but something that is given, and understanding this is what makes us godly and begins to make us God-like.

As with all of the greatest gifts, like love and faith and peace, gratitude grows as it is given, and its concepts can be joyfully studied forever. Each thing we learn of it suggests two things we do not yet understand, and the pursuit of gratitude, like the pursuit of joy, can go on forever and is the essence of what people of faith might call eternal progression.

Yet while it takes forever, its blessings and benefits begin to manifest themselves the minute we make gratitude our goal. Living in the atmosphere of gratitude can start whenever we want it to start. Gratitude is a gift that is always available. All we have to do is learn how to practice it and how to receive it.

We can cultivate the joy that comes in moments—capture them—the eye-rolling happiness of a child's kiss; the unexcelled, unparalleled joy of new life—the moments that make everything else worth it.

A Transforming Skill and a Heavenly Gift

Rabbi Harold Kushner suggested that all it takes to have gratitude is concentration:

Can you see the holiness in those things you take for granted—a paved road or a washing machine? If you concentrate on finding what is good in every situation,

We need to learn to live in thanksgiving—to make it our atmosphere—to be surrounded by it—to let it permeate everything.

Within gratitude's atmosphere, pride cannot survive. Enmity cannot live. Neither condescension nor envy can breathe.

How do we live in thanksgiving? How do we cloak ourselves with gratitude?

How, in the demanding and sometimes desperate walk of the everyday, do we remember that we are living in God's light, that we breathe according to His will, that our very lives and everything in them are His gifts?

you will discover that your life will suddenly be filled with gratitude, a feeling that nurtures the soul.

As we gradually develop the habit of gratitude, we see blessings all around, in and a part of everything. In the light of our awareness, gifts elongate like sun-setting shadows.

Basic gratitude is a skill we can learn, through concentration and practice.

If it is learned well enough, practiced long enough, it can become an attitude and an atmosphere, with which and in which we live—and live more fully.

Gratitude is an element that, though often hidden, is always present, at least in traces, in every experience, every moment. Finding it, feeling it, and giving it is what we can practice.

Once located—a skill we can become good at—gratitude is compatible, even symbiotic, with every other emotion, and can shape-shift them all into something calmer, sweeter.

Irritation and annoyance with an adversary can transform—into gratitude for new awareness of another perspective.

Disappointment with the weather can transform—into gratitude for variety and unpredictable surprise and appreciation of beauty.

Fear of things we can't control or predict can transform—into gratitude for serendipity.

Boredom with routine can transform—into gratitude for stability and safety.

Vague appreciation for comfort and ease can transform—into gratitude for small specifics like a storm window or a car that starts.

Even frustration with traffic and potholes can transform—into gratitude for the government (imagine that) and the roads built for us.

Gratitude is better than appreciation. The latter might be nothing more than politeness, while the former has depth of feeling and expression.

Thanks-giving can become a skill, an aptitude, a talent, defined and deliberate and directed—developed by awareness, perspective, and practice. It can be generated, gained, and given, and it is, as much as we want of it, within our power.

But that kind of thankfulness, our own earned and practiced kind, is only the beginning of gratitude.

There is a higher form, one in which our only proactive part is requesting, recognizing, and receiving. This is the higher, yet deeper, gratitude that is a gift from God.

It is different not just in degree, but in kind. It comes from without, not from within and it wells in our spirits, not our emotions.

We will learn more of this gratitude together in this book, but it is not within our power, only within God's. And we cannot earn it, only ask for it.

Consciously or not,
whenever we feel
gratitude for something,
we feel it to someone.

The two types are connected. Gratitude as a skill precedes, precipitates, and pulls gratitude as a gift.

Consciously or not, whenever we feel gratitude for something, we feel it to someone.

And, accept it or not, that someone is ultimately God. Thus, as we practice, we, aware or not, draw nearer to Him, and begin to receive more of His gift.

At one time or another, we all sense, unverbalized, that we were once in an earlier place, with a God we called Father. His gift to us was this earth, this chance to explore.

As we work on the skill of gratitude, gradually, a higher talent is revealed—the spiritual skill of knowing what to ask for and the understanding of how to receive it.

The Skills That Make Up the Skill

An aptitude for gratitude does not come by itself. It is a combination of other skills. To get "good at gratitude" we need to get good at noticing and awareness, good at humility, good at expressing thanks, good at remembering, good at receiving.

The middle part and central core of this book is about the skills that make up the skill, and about how each of them connects to the ultimate skill and gift of gratitude.

The joy of these connections is that they feed each other and motivate each other. Getting better at awareness makes us better at gratitude, and feeling more thankfulness makes us more aware. Understanding grace feeds directly into the gratitude we feel, and then that added appreciation expands our grasp of grace.

We have identified—and experimented with—twelve qualities that we believe are components of gratitude, twelve skills that make up the skill.

Start anytime during the year with the idea of working on one of the components each month, thus arriving at the next Thanksgiving better equipped to feel more joy-giving gratitude than the year before.

And the progression is like an upward spiral. More love prompts more gratitude, which then finds more love. With each of the twelve complementing qualities, the arrow goes both ways between it and gratitude—increasing one increases the other.

Poetry instead of Prose

As we began sending out Thanksgiving greetings each year, we realized something: Poetry is better than prose when it comes to talking about thanks-giving. Gratitude is a feeling, and poetry is the language of feelings. Thanks-giving is more an art than a science, and poems and verse express it better than numbers or sentences and paragraphs.

This book now makes that shift, going forward with the broken lines and the mind-suggestions and brevity of poetry and semi-poetry.

Don't be put off by the shift. Read more for the feeling than the logic, more for the music than the lyrics. See what the poetry can do to you rather than what you can do to the poetry. Follow the advice that America's Poet Laureate Billy Collins gives his readers:

> *I ask them to take a poem*
> *and hold it up to the light*
> *like a color slide . . .*

Rather than

> *. . . beating it with a hose*
> *to find out what it really means.*

The best way to expand gratitude is to make connections.
As one bubble bumps another and jumps instantly
into a doubled bubble,
So can gratitude bump awareness, or love, or health,
And instantly expand itself.
These twelve short chapters are each on one of the connections,
And they are mostly descriptive and conceptual,
But they each end with an "exercise" that will help you
Bring about the bump and create the connection.

PART TWO

EXPANDING THANKS-GIVING THROUGH THE WHOLE YEAR

A TRADITION, A SKILL, A GIFT, AND A CONNECTION TO JOY

Here's a suggestion that will help in the bumping:

Get a nice-feel book of blank paper in which to

Perform these simple exercises.

Call it a "gratitude journal" if you wish. We will call it "your book."

It will help you keep track of gratitude—so that next Thanksgiving,

You will live more deeply within it.

CHALLENGE: Do the exercise every month (you can start any month)

PROMISE: "Your book" will mean far more to you by next Thanksgiving than this book.

Perhaps nothing helps us make the movement from our little selves to a larger world than remembering God in gratitude.
—Henri Nouwen

To look backward for a while is to refresh the eye, to restore it, and to render it the more fit for its prime function of looking forward.
—Margaret Fairless Barber, *The Roadmender*

NOVEMBER

THANKS-GIVING & REMEMBRANCE

The most fortunate are those who have a wonderful capacity to appreciate again and again, freshly and naively, the basic goods of life, with awe, pleasure, wonder, and even ecstasy.

ABRAHAM MASLOW

Y et . . .

Most human beings have an almost infinite capacity for taking things for granted.

ALDOUS HUXLEY

It is all about remembering our blessings.

There are certain perfect late-autumn days that
Lend themselves to reflection and remembering.
The certainty of winter induces fond recall
Of longer, warmer days, and
The sky spreads wide like a mackerel memory,
Its bright scales revealing the reeds of past deeds,
The peace of earlier release.

As we approach the holiday that is
Named after the synonym for happiness,
The build-up should be about remembering.
The year now winding down, we look back
And recall how much has been given us,
And how little we deserve it.

Remembering may be the precise opposite
Of taking-for-granted.
Some say that remembering is the consummate skill.
When we remember,
We don't have to learn the same facts,
Or the same lessons, or the same abilities
All over again.
When we remember,
We return favors and thank people for small things.
When we remember, it makes God bigger
And ourselves comfortably, securely smaller.

When we remember moments of joy,
The moments are twice felt.

When we remember error,
We are less likely to repeat it.
When we remember love, it is nourished and grows.
When we remember peace,
We also remember where to find it.

And when we remember gratitude, it overflows,
Leaving us warmed and filled.

We nurture and care for our gratitude by remembering,
Negotiating the curbs and trips of takeforgranted
That could spill the beauty from the buggy.

There are many ways to remember to be grateful,
The best one being prayer.
Pray oftener,
And give equal content-weight to prayer's two sides:
Thanking and Asking.

Remembering is both a bridge and a mirror,
Showing us where and who we are
and who we have become.

These are good things to think about
As the year winds down,
And the grace of Christmas ramps up.

CHALLENGE:

In your book,
(did you get your book, as suggested four pages back?)
As Thanksgiving approaches, start a list
Of thankful things big and small.
Number it.
1. Sunsets, 2. Doorknobs, 3. A mother's love, 4. . . .
It may range from the petty to the profound.
On Thanksgiving morning, while the turkey cooks,
Build the list. Get everyone involved.
See if you can get to 100, 200, 500 . . .
Think for a moment about each one,
About why you are happy to have it.
Let each tiny twinge of gratitude collect in your list
To help you Remember.

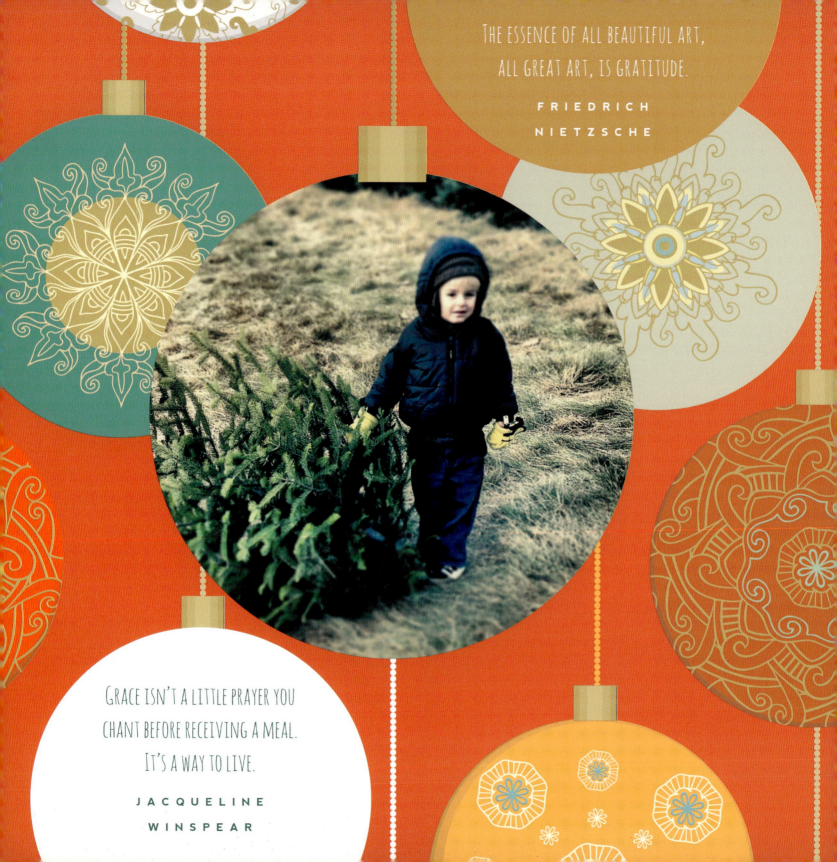

The essence of all beautiful art, all great art, is gratitude.

FRIEDRICH NIETZSCHE

Grace isn't a little prayer you chant before receiving a meal. It's a way to live.

JACQUELINE WINSPEAR

DECEMBER

THANKS-GIVING & GRACE

WHEN WE WERE CHILDREN WE WERE GRATEFUL TO THOSE WHO FILLED OUR STOCKINGS AT CHRISTMAS TIME. WHY ARE WE NOT GRATEFUL TO GOD FOR FILLING OUR STOCKINGS WITH LEGS?   G. K. CHESTERTON

It is all for your sake, so that as grace extends to more and more people it may increase thanksgiving, to the glory of God.

2 CORINTHIANS 4:15

Perhaps gratitude, grace, and joy
All begin with beauty.
Keats said, "A thing of beauty is a joy forever,"
And then he upped the ante by saying,
"Beauty is truth, truth beauty.
That is all ye know on earth,
And all ye need to know."

In the rant and rush of pushy life,
We need to find the moments,
To see beauty,
To sit peacefully and feel our thoughts,
And soak in the gratitude and grace and joy.

Grace and Gratitude go together,
Not only in their alliteration,
But in their root—both come from the Latin "gratia"
Meaning grace, graciousness, or gratefulness.
Grace is the ultimate gratitude to the Ultimate Giver.

A beauty from within.

Destined to fly onward through space
Without an end or a destination—
A circuit without a current,
An expression without a connection.

But to say "I'm thankful" to the giver completes the circuit
And turns on the light,
Especially if the Giver is God and the Light is His Spirit.

Christmas, the wave of beauty and peace,
The celebration of the birth of stunning sacrifice . . .
We are as a tiny naked babe staring up and
Trying to grasp the grandeur of His grace.

"Grace-full-ness"
Amazing Grace
Beyond amazing, grace is
Miraculously mysterious because
It is the magic of One Spirit's singular perfection
Overcoming the vast imperfections of the other billions.

If thanks just lies there, naked and inert,
It will probably fossilize and turn hard and brittle.
By itself it is unconnected
And spinning in its own lonely orbit.
It needs to be applied to something
And extended to someone.

To say "I'm thankful" as an observation is one thing,
But to point and say "I'm thankful" for that blessing
And to let a little place in you turn warm and quiver a bit
With the beauty of it . . .
That is thankfulness with an object.

Still, without a recipient or a subject,
The thanks is sterile and undirected,

We can't comprehend it, but we can appreciate it
And be awed by it.
And peace somehow interprets itself within us,
Changing us, transforming us, gradually gifting grace
Until we become grace-full and grateful,
A beauty from within.

Gratitude plays a place in the transformation—
Growing, gathering perspective and awareness,
Deepening and permeating and in a way overwhelming us
Into realizing that it is actually too big
For mere appreciation to comprehend.

Evolving, elevating, energizing,
A progressing process whereby gratitude turns to awe
And finally to grace.
And we emerge amazed and awe-struck and saved.
Gratitude beyond gratitude!

The Biblical Paul taught us that it is by grace (God's gift)
That we are saved, after all we can do.

 CHALLENGE:

However you pray, add more thanks-giving.
Thank God for 5 new things each night.
In your book, keep a list for the month—
"The 31 days of Christmas"
Then, on New Year's Eve, inventory all 155.

Wake at dawn with a winged heart
and give thanks for another day of
loving. —KAHLIL GIBRAN

JANUARY

THANKS-GIVING & PERSPECTIVE

WE CAN ONLY BE SAID TO BE ALIVE IN THOSE MOMENTS WHEN OUR HEARTS ARE CONSCIOUS OF OUR TREASURES. **THORNTON WILDER**

Clearly, one of the major obstacles to our experience of gratitude is the habit we have of sleepwalking through life. The truth is that we are never lacking for blessings in our lives, but we are often lacking in awareness and recognition of them.

DIANE BERKE, PH.D

In every thing give thanks: for this is the will of God.

1 THESSALONIANS 5:18

Our seeing is improved,
Not so much by a new ocular prescription
As by increasing awareness and perspective.
With deliberate effort, we can open our minds to light
And become as one bird, alight, but with winged heart,
Feeling the world all around and able to fly up
And see it all from above.

Can you state the difference between man and God
In two words?
Is to ask, or to try, blasphemous?
If we did attempt, the two words might be:
Awareness and Perspective.

We have infinitely more in common than different.

We see such a narrow slice, a sliver really,
God sees all.
Our perspective is earthly and mortal,
His is eternal and perfect.

What saves us is awareness and our perspective
And both are expandable
And we sense that, as His children,
We have infinitely more in common than different.

Awareness . . .
We have five senses, and use only a fraction of each.
And a sixth, in the soul, often dormant
But always summon-able.

Were we all more aware, we would all be more grateful,
For awareness is the sense and perception
Of what is around us and in us,

And the epiphany that all of both come from God.
Those who see that, who really see it,
Also see God.
The shortest perspective is
Eat, drink, and be merry,
But that kind of merriness never turns to joy.

A middle perspective is duty,
And while it keeps commandments and follows laws,
It does not, now or ever, exalt the soul.

The longest perspective is eternity,
And oh how that perspective changes us.
Extending our view from finite to infinite, letting us
See suddenly that we are not growing up from the earth,
But hanging down from the sky.

A two-way eternity, not only forever forward,
But forever back into pre-mortal life
Where we, full of perspective,
Shouted for joy at the prospect
Of coming to this physical place
To struggle and fumble and fizzle and fail
But to learn from it all, to progress in ways not possible
Until body and agency and families of our own
Made us more like God.

That perspective precipitates and promotes and produces
Gratitude.
How could it not, because it presupposes a Father-God
Who wants to give us all He has.

❤▷ CHALLENGE:

Wake up!

Notice more!

Take more in!

Spend less time inside yourself, worrying,

And more time outside yourself, rejoicing.

If you have troubles, see through them.

If you have challenges, see over them.

If you have blessings, see God's hand in them.

This month, taste, smell, look, and listen harder,

And feel more, with both your skin and your soul.

In your book, each day, write down one new thing

That one of your senses revealed to you

And let your increasing awareness give you

The perspective

That catalyzes gratitude.

Love must be as much a light as it is a flame.

—HENRY DAVID THOREAU

FEBRUARY

THANKS-GIVING & LOVE

Can you look at beauty and frame it with a heart,
So that both thanks and love ride easily
Upon the seeing?
Can love and gratitude rise high in parallel planes?
So emotion's energy
Can flicker back and forth between them,
Multiplying each other like chicken and egg?

Gratitude, like love, grows every time it is given
Or received.
In fact, ask yourself,

Are Thanks-Giving and Love separable?
Can we feel one without feeling the other?
Or are they intertwined so completely
That it is impossible to tell
Where one ends and the other begins?

We all need love and we all need to give love.
We need someone to comfort us
And to hold our head when it hurts,
And when it doesn't, we need to be the holder.

> # LOVE IS THE MASTER KEY THAT OPENS THE GATES OF HAPPINESS.
>
> OLIVER WENDELL HOLMES

Some say *love* is such a special word that perhaps
We should not use it so much,
On the premise that, if you try to love everything,
You will end up loving nothing

The other view is that *love* is such a special word
That we should use it every minute . . .
That love breeds more love and is inexhaustible
And infinitely expandable.
There are more things to love than we can ever find.
You might love one percent
Of all the things you could have loved this day
And every time you add another, gratitude grows.

You are, as one, limited and isolated;
Your slice of reality is just a sliver,
But to love others gets you into their heads
and you see what they have seen

Like entering different crystal balls,
One after another.
We need to learn to love like brothers, sisters,
And like friends,
And like parents,
And like children,
And like lovers and partners.

Here is some more magic:
As we get better at remembering blessings,
It is guaranteed
That we will also become more generous.
It is not possible to become better at receiving
Without also becoming better at giving,
Because they are two sides of one coin
And, put in motion, they spin up, feeding each other,
Catching the sun,
Reaching a higher realm of love.

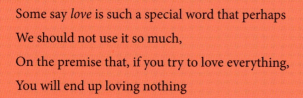

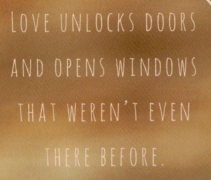

Love unlocks doors
and opens windows
that weren't even
there before.

MIGNON MCLAUGHLIN

 CHALLENGE:

In this Valentine's month,
Love something or someone new each day.
A new-noticed beauty, a small opportunity,
A little convenience,
Or a person you have never loved before.
Write one in your book each day.
Many will be the same things you have felt grateful for,
But this time, say "I love you."

MARCH

THANKS-GIVING & CHARACTER

GRATITUDE IS THE SIGN OF NOBLE SOULS.   AESOP

There is no greater difference between men than between grateful and ungrateful people.

R.H. BLYTHE

Not only can gratitude make us happy, it can make us good.
It can give us the courage to hold out our hand,
For there is no darkness in gratitude
And no light in its absence.

How can we comprehend this more clearly?
Try wadding up all bads into one wrap, labeled "self":
Selfish, Self-centered, Self-absorbed, Self-congratulating . . .
And notice that someone all wrapped up in himself
Makes a very small package.

Then on the opposite side of the box:
Empathy, humility, love, courage, honesty . . .
All flowing from gratitude.

Then on the other side of the spectrum: Empathy, humility, love, courage, honesty . . . . all flowing from **GRATITUDE.**

Thanks and love,
One and one, one on one—each day
Say "thank you" to someone. Not polite and perfunctory,
But eye-to-eye, or at least heart to heart,
feeling it, meaning it.

Record the receiver's name, each day of the month,
In your book.

Can you think of an evil person who was grateful?
Or of a proud, unappreciative one who was good?
Could it be that the mere practice of thanks-giving,
The deliberate effort to see through a gratitude lens,
Makes bad men good and good men better?
And gives us the honesty to be exactly who we are?

It is intuitive to know that loving more and thanking more
Lifts the receiver even as it builds the giver.
But just thinking about it won't do it.
It is the application that brings the accumulation.
Outflowing love and thanks creates the inflow
Of character.

GRATITUDE IS THE GREATEST OF VIRTUES, IN FACT, THE PARENT OF ALL OTHER VIRTUES.

CICERO

NOTHING IS MORE HONORABLE THAN A GRATEFUL HEART. SENECA

THANKS-GIVING GIVES US THE HONESTY TO BE EXACTLY WHO WE ARE.

And what foolish child would not avail himself of
the source of exploding sunsets?

"Asking the right questions
takes as much skill as
giving the right answers."
—Robert Half

APRIL

THANKS-GIVING & ASKING

I WOULD RATHER BE ABLE TO APPRECIATE THINGS I CANNOT HAVE THAN
TO HAVE THINGS I AM NOT ABLE TO APPRECIATE.

ELBERT HUBBARD

If you are a parent, you want your children to ask.
Because the more they ask, the more likely they will be
To receive what you give.

And a wise child learns that to ask is to praise,
Which prompts the parent to give more.

The same equation and chemistry applies
With the parent that we call God,
And what foolish child would not avail himself
Of the source of exploding sunsets.

Asking is not the opposite of thanks-giving.
It is the complement and the other half of the formula.
Christ always coupled the equation:
"Ask and Receive."

In His universe (and it is His)
There is agency, and since that is His gift,
He does not violate it. If He were to
Take the initiative and simply give us what we need,
And what He would like to give (everything He has)

It would pilfer our agency and leave us
As dependent dole-dwellers.

So He commands "ask" because that is our initiative,
And the exercise of our agency
Leaves Him free to give without robbing
And to enrich our lives without impoverishing our will.

Some say "Don't ask too much" or "Don't ask for too much."
We say ask more and ask for more,
Because that is what God says, repeatedly, in holy writ.

"Ask"—may be the most frequently repeated admonition
In all of scripture.

Is redundancy a way of drumming its necessity?
Could failure to follow
Become our greatest eternal embarrassment?

But some children, asking constantly,
Prompt a parent to start saying "no."
Is it the same with God,
Or is there a built-in re-route switch
That circles our prayer back and alters and adjusts it,
Causing us to ask just what He wants us to,
Unlocking the very door He wants us to pass through,
Almost always a surprise;
And almost always, at least with later perspective,
Better.

Sometimes the best way to start is to just sit still,
cup your face, and relish the answers.

Be it God or one of His parent children,
There are some things no one gets tired of being asked:
Advice, Opinion, Input, Suggestions, Honest Questions.

Is asking weak, an admission of need, of dependency?
("If I have to ask directions, it admits I'm lost.")
No, it is the strong, honest, humble vulnerability
That invites love so that
Sometimes when we pray, our hearts know we are heard,
As though a hole opened into heaven.

ASK, AND YE SHALL RECEIVE. NEW TESTAMENT

ASKING IS THE BEGINNING OF RECEIVING. MAKE SURE YOU DON'T GO TO THE OCEAN WITH A TEASPOON.

JIM ROHN

CHALLENGE:

So this month, practice asking.

Practice the creative formulation of a good question.

Ask someone something, every day this month and

In prayer, ask for one thing you truly think you need.

Write each day's mortal and divine question in your book,

Along with the answers you receive.

Notice the improvement in questions and answers

by month's end.

There are times when blessings swirl down like a flurry of blossoms . . .

MAY

THANKS-GIVING & RECEIVING

The unthankful heart . . . discovers no mercies; but let the thankful heart sweep through the day and, as the magnet finds the iron, so it will find, in every hour, some heavenly blessings!

HENRY WARD BEECHER

Taste is nothing but an enlarged capacity for receiving pleasure from works of imagination.

WILLIAM HAZLETT

Hem your blessings with thankfulness so they don't unravel.

UNKNOWN

Life ebbs and flows,
And at times the heavens seem to withdraw and withhold.
But there are other times when blessings swirl down
Like a flurry of blossoms and
We can neither grasp nor see them all.

But in feast and in famine, we need to learn how to receive.

Even in football, where Quarterbacks get the headlines,

None succeed without a good receiver.
No matter how perfect the pass,
Nothing counts if the receiver drops the ball.
Good receivers reach out and pull in,
Even as opposition swipes and bumps.

Good receivers never take the pass for granted
Or assume it will be easy to catch.
They expect difficulty and deal with it,
And they see the virtue even in a wobbly pass.

They are ready to run new routes and to adjust old ones
According to where the opposition lines up.
The more the receiver wants the ball and the more he
Shows his willingness to do whatever it takes to catch it,
The more the quarterback will pass to him.

The physics law says
Every action has an equal and opposite reaction.
Is there a corresponding spiritual law? Can there be?

In this world we borrow and owe and repay,
But we cannot repay heaven.

How do you repay breath or time or nature?
Are we hopelessly and eternally indebted?
And what could we return anyway?
What would you use as currency to pay back life?
As blessings come down, what can we send back up?

The only currency we have is thanks,
And maybe that will do . . . simply because the Lender
Already has everything else.
Perhaps our thanks is the appropriate and best return,
Since it is the only thing we have to give and the only thing
He does not have.

Receiving is a whole thing, an eternal round, encompassing.
Accept it all: The timing, The unexpected, The challenge
Never second-guessing, never doubting, never resenting—
Sometimes then, a flood of providence is unleashed,
Flowing unrestrained over every part of our world.

Ask and receive, give and take. Thus hold life in balance.
You will die if you don't take in a breath,
and you will die if you don't let it out.
All giving and no receiving may bring exhaustion,
Or resentment, or depression.
But all receiving and no giving is selfishness and entitlement.

In a universe where God owns all, receiving
Is more important than accomplishing and
Returning thanks is part of the celestial formula for returning.

Practice, persist,
Until receiving becomes an art, applicable equally
To the jewels around your neck or those clustered on a leaf.

❤ CHALLENGE:

Send or deliver one hand-written note of thanks
Each week this month.
That alone will make you a unique receiver.
And since receiving is partly about accepting the
Balance between pleasure and pain,
In your book, each day, write two things:
The best and the worst, the happy and the sad.
Practice accepting them both, treating them both the same,
Finding some sliver or lining of joy in each.

The light, the game, the vitality . . .

GRATITUDE UNLOCKS THE FULLNESS OF LIFE. IT TURNS WHAT WE HAVE INTO ENOUGH, AND MORE. IT TURNS DENIAL INTO ACCEPTANCE, CHAOS INTO ORDER, AND CONFUSION INTO CLARITY. . . . IT TURNS PROBLEMS INTO GIFTS, FAILURES INTO SUCCESS, THE UNEXPECTED INTO PERFECT TIMING, AND MISTAKES INTO IMPORTANT EVENTS. GRATITUDE MAKES SENSE OF OUR PAST, BRINGS PEACE FOR TODAY, AND CREATES A VISION FOR TOMORROW. MELODIE BEATTIE

JUNE

◆

THANKS-GIVING & HEALTH/VITALITY

Love cures people—both the ones who give it and the ones who receive it.

KARL MENNINGER

Gratitude is a vaccine, an antitoxin, and an antiseptic.

JOHN HENRY JOWETT

Every one of our greatest national treasures, our liberty, enterprise, vitality, wealth, military power, global authority, flow from a surprising sorce: our ability to give thanks.

TONY SNOW

Gratitude is no passive lay-back,
It is a proactive grasp. Wherever you are,
Spin your head and count the blessings, the beach,
the light, the game, the vitality.

Popular phrase: "reinventing ourselves."
It might mean looking more deeply for our gifts
and our destinies.

But perhaps the best thing we can reinvent ourselves into
Is an always grateful person.
Which may prove to be the very fountain of vitality.

Vitality is health.
It is also purpose and meaning.
It is also thanks-giving.
For gratitude breeds vision and vigor and well-being
Which energizes and balances, inoculating against
The dark ills of depression and despair.

Jumping high, through the world . . .

Gratitude is a positive emotion that strengthens its vessel.
A self-fulfilling prophecy
That seems to return more of whatever we give thanks for.

There is an abundance in gratitude, a billowing fullness
That warms and lifts us
And causes our bodies to respond with vigor,
Jumping high, through the world.

Besides fuel and rest, body well-being requires two things:
The exercise that tones the muscles and mind,
And the relaxation that calms them.

Gratitude can't do much directly for the former,
Although appreciation for activity may increase it,
But it can motivate and enhance the latter like nothing else.

Meditation or yoga or any kind of relaxation response
Is colored and textured by gratitude.

Especially if you alter your practice a bit. . . .

Instead of focusing on an object, focus on a blessing.
Instead of thinking about your breath,
Think with gratitude for air and lung.
Make "Thank You" your mantra

And the next time you hear about the proliferation of
Stress-induced illness,
You can counter it with your personal preservation of
Gratitude-induced vitality.

◐ CHALLENGE:

This month, once each day, anytime,

Pause.

Sit still and serene,

Relax and loosen wrists and ankles and

Let it spread from there.

Then focus for three minutes

On one simple, visualize-able blessing.

See it in your mind from all perspectives.

Block every other thought.

Later that day, write it in your book.

The one that lights our eye . . .

. . . and the children who light our lives.

Without humility it is impossible to enjoy anything, even pride.
—G.K. Chesterton

JULY

THANKS-GIVING & FAMILY

How wonderful it would be if we could help our children and grandchildren to learn thanksgiving at an early age. Thanksgiving opens the doors. It changes a child's personality. . . . Thankful children want to give, they radiate happiness, they draw people.

SIR JOHN TEMPLETON

How sharper than a serpent's tooth it is to have a thankless child!

SHAKESPEARE, *KING LEAR*

When written in Chinese, the word crisis *is composed of two characters—one represents danger, and the other represents opportunity.*

JOHN F. KENNEDY

Gratitude radiates from family like sparks from flint and steel,
The One who lights our eye,
and the children that light our lives.

No family is perfect,
All families have challenges, but
Commitment is what cements family joy. . . .
As we grasp the foreverness of family and feel
The security of saying "It is you, and it will always be you."
Gratitude floods in.

The harsh uncertainty of the outside world
Is neutralized by the sureness and security
Of the inside home
Where we celebrate commitment and popularize parenting
And validate values.

Then we venture forth strong into the outer
Because of the inner gratitude we carry always with us.

For partners, thanks-giving's lens focuses light,
White hot, on the precise center of the gratitude bulls eye.
The One. Our other half. The burning focal point of love,
The blessing above all blessings.

Saying "I love you more than all else, and more than myself"
Is like saying "My ultimate thanks is for you and to you."
No greater love, no greater gratitude.
Neither can be said too often.
And nothing can provide more power and more peace.

For parents, thanks-giving
Is not only our reward but our methodology
Because gratitude is the antidote to the entitlement attitudes
That would destroy our families and our kids.

Children, particularly young, unspoiled ones,
Possess the natural gift of gratitude—but it is unlit.
We can spark it, not by telling them to say thank you
But by letting them see us say it, repeatedly, all day,
To friends, to teachers, to God, and even to them.

The more they hear you say it,
And see your happiness as you do,
The more they will emulate both the saying and the feeling.

Start with the conscious realization that family matters most.
Real Eyes that most things we do are merely the means
For the same end.
And that end is family.

Sort the means from the ends with one simple question:

"Why?"

Why do you work? Why do you strive?

Why do you pray? Why do you eat? Why do you care?

Ultimately, the answer to every why is "family."

Would there be a parallel ratio between how much

You value a thing and how grateful you are for it?

(Level of importance proportionate to level of thanks?)

If so, no contest. We are most grateful for family.

But gratitude and joy do not linger like a heavy blanket,

Rather they come in flashes, in moments,

And we recognize them as a gleam in the eye.

 CHALLENGE:

This month, in your book,

Guided by your imagination and your hope,

Write a one-paragraph description of your relationship

With each member of your family five years from now.

This is relationship goal-setting,

And it can become self-fulfilling, a verbal magnet

That pulls reality

And sparks the most personal gratitude of all.

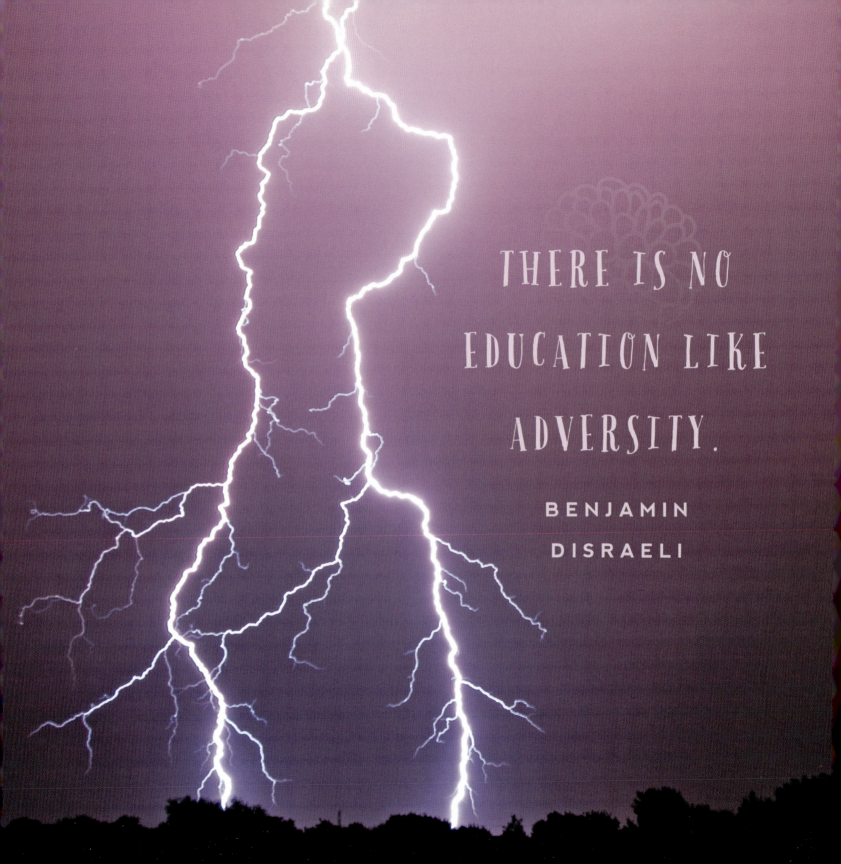

AUGUST

THANKS-GIVING & ADVERSITY

> Being mistreated is the most important condition of mortality, for eternity itself depends on how we view those who mistreat us.
>
> JAMES L. FERRELL

When it is dark enough, you can see the stars.

RALPH WALDO EMERSON

If I had a formula for bypassing trouble, I would not pass it round. Trouble creates a capacity to handle it. I don't embrace trouble; that's as bad as treating it as an enemy. But I do say meet it as a friend, for you will see a lot of it, and had better be on speaking terms with it.

OLIVER WENDELL HOLMES

Many of us, with the blessing of hindsight, say
Thank you for adversity and conclude
that the greatest moments were when lightning struck.

Looking back, we can see
How something we thought was horrible and unfair
Turned out to be a great blessing.

The trick is to see it that way right away!

Adversity projects its
own kind of beauty,
Too hot to touch, but
Bathing our faces in
flickering light.

Other times we see it in
the corner of our eye.

In a sense, adversity is essential to gratitude.
If there were none of one there would be none of the other.
Light can't be seen without the contrast of dark.

Adversity projects its own kind of beauty,
Too hot to touch, but
Bathing our faces in flickering light,
Helping us to understand how strong and how beautiful
We really are.

Sometimes it hits us in the face,
And other times we see it coming out of the corner of our eye.

There are two correct responses to adversity
Depending on its nature.
One is to fight it and change it and win out over it.
The other is to accept it and summon gratitude for it.
Separating the two
Is one of the most valuable skills in life;
Some people call it "picking your battles."

Sometimes the mere act of being thankful for adversity
Takes the sting out of it.
Whistle while you work. Sing as you march into battle.
A little known Biblical king, Josiah, overshadowed by
Luminaries like David and Solomon, practiced this with success.
When a large allied army swept down on tiny Israel,
Josiah placed his choir at the front of his army, singing,
"Give thanks to the Lord for he is good.
His mercy endures forever."
The opposing force became disoriented and fled in terror.

Adversity is the best atmosphere in which to practice gratitude
. . . like the resistance on the treadmill
. . . like a kite rising against the wind.

CHALLENGE:

This month, actually audit your adversity,
Not to emphasize the negative,
But to prove to yourself that it's a necessary part
that is always there.
Instead of hoping to be rid of it,
Make peace with it, and hone the art of overcoming.
In your book, each day,
Note some little obstacle you faced,
And write how you either got past it
Or made friends with it.

GRATITUDE SHIFTS YOUR FOCUS FROM
WHAT YOUR LIFE LACKS TO THE
ABUNDANCE THAT IS ALREADY PRESENT.

MARELISA FABREGA

SEPTEMBER

THANKS-GIVING & SERENDIPITY/STEWARDSHIP

GRATITUDE IS A QUALITY SIMILAR TO ELECTRICITY. IT MUST BE PRODUCED AND DISCHARGED AND USED UP IN ORDER TO EXIST AT ALL.

WILLIAM FAULKNER

It is literally true, as the thankless say, that they have nothing to be thankful for. He who sits by the fire, thankless for the fire, is just as if he had no fire. Nothing is possessed save in appreciation, of which thankfulness is the indispensable ingredient. But a thankful heart hath a continual feast.

W. J. CAMERON

The robbed that smiles steals something from the thief.

SHAKESPEARE. *OTHELLO*

We often resist something that we should relish
And be grateful for.
It is the unexpected.
Surprise, well accepted, is the spice and savor of life.
Not knowing where the river winds or
Where the day will take you is a reality
That we might as well convert into a joy.

And, opposite, we often relish something that we should resist.
It is the notion of ownership.
We don't own anything, except perhaps our agency.
All else passes through our hands, owned only by God
And loaned to us on trial.

As much as we might think we want control,
The best we can hope for is serendipity,
And our misplaced pursuit of ownership
Converts with wisdom to stewardship.
Together, these two 11-letter "S" words
Give us a guided glimpse of divine gratitude.

Serendipity and Stewardship, like Scripture, tell us to focus
On Watching and Praying at least as much as on
Working and Planning, because
Along will come something better than
What we thought we pursued;
And while nothing is ours, all is given to us.

Thus real joy comes not just in the striving
But in the accepting,
And sometimes just to leap and soar,
Trusting that you will land where you should.

Let's push back the Working and Planning,
And the other Worldly and Posturing W and P words
Worry and Pursue
Wealth and Power, and even
Writing and Prose.

To make room for a new gratitude-freshened W and P set:
Watch and Pray
Wander and Ponder
Wonder and Probe
Worship and Praise
Waken and Perceive
Wait and Procrastinate (selectively)
Weigh and Perspective
Wisdom and Peace, and even
Watching and Poetry

Then, like a steward, we will begin to see serendipity,
Then, like a baby, we will crawl pleasantly
Into the unknown.

 **CHALLENGE:**

Give up on control.
Write down in your book each day something that
You are glad you don't consciously control
From things as internally automatic as digestion or
Your tear ducts or sweat glands—
To something as unpredictably external as weather
Or sunsets.
Think how glad you are to observe and enjoy and benefit
Rather than controlling them all.

We will crawl pleasantly into the unknown.

RELAX AND JUST BE WHO YOU ARE.

OCTOBER

THANKS-GIVING & THE CONFIDENT HUMILITY OF FAITH

I AM NOTHING; I AM BUT AN INSTRUMENT, A TINY PENCIL IN THE HANDS OF THE LORD WITH WHICH HE WRITES WHAT HE LIKES. HOWEVER IMPERFECT WE ARE, HE WRITES BEAUTIFULLY.

MOTHER TERESA

The earth is the Lord's and everything in it.

PSALMS 24:1

Behold the graciousness and generosity of God, who wants people to be able to have life, and live it to the full. Not, however, at the expense of forgetting to whom it all belongs.

BEN WITHERINGTON III IN *JESUS AND MONEY*

God has two dwellings: one in heaven, and the other in a meek and thankful heart.

IZAAK WALTON

The acceptance of God as the Giver
Makes us strive for excellence, but also
Allows us to relax and just be who we are.

Among other wonders is the wonder of smallness—
The miracle that we are exactly the right size for the earth.
We fit the scale.
Were we bigger or smaller,
We would not work well with this world.
Spiritually it is the same—

As His creations, we are among the tiniest,
As His children, we are of largest import and consequence.

It is somewhat sad
That two symbiotic, nearly synonymous words
Are thought of as opposites. . . .
Humility and confidence look like each other's antithesis
Until their common source—our relationship to God—
is revealed and they
Coalesce into closeness and simpatico,
Pushed together by perspective, and by
A father who helps us stand.

If we call God "Father," and mean it,
We merit inescapable, inherited confidence,
Yet His perfection's vast distance from our foibles
Creates profound humility

A relaxing quality that puts the pressure off of you
And the yoke on Him.

The message: Stop stressing and start praying.

To a Christian, there is one form of thanks
That supersedes and overpowers all others.
It is the unspeakable, un-repayable, unfathomable gratitude
We feel to a Savior who has literally purchased us
With His blood.

Somehow—some ungraspable how—
He had amassed enough spiritual capital
To ransom us, to pay the staggering debt of our
Collective sin and error
And allow us to escape the debtors prison into which
We would otherwise find ourselves eternally confined.

One reason this gratitude goes beyond all others
Is that Christ's ultimate gift is something that neither we,
Nor anyone else who has ever lived,
Could have done for ourselves.

And while we cannot fully comprehend it,
We can stand in awe, which is the ultimate gratitude.
As C. S. Lewis said, "Beware of professed Christians
Who posses insufficient awe of Christ."

Or as Neal A. Maxwell expanded, "The more we ponder
Where we stand in relation to Jesus Christ,
The more we realize
That we do not stand at all, we only kneel."

Without this gift, our lives would be much like
A diminishing road into a growing fog,
Or like a dying red sun setting in for the last time.
But with His gift, the fog dissipates, the sun rises again,
And we are free to recover, time and time again
And to continually partake of all the lesser blessings.

 CHALLENGE:

Cultivate a positive "can't do" attitude.
Oxymoron?
No, because the can't do is the realistic humility
Of how inconsequential we are,
While the positive is the spiritualistic faith
Of how God can do with us and through us, anything.
Each day write down in your book,
Something you have that you don't deserve and didn't earn.
This, by the way,
Is the very easiest of all twelve challenges.

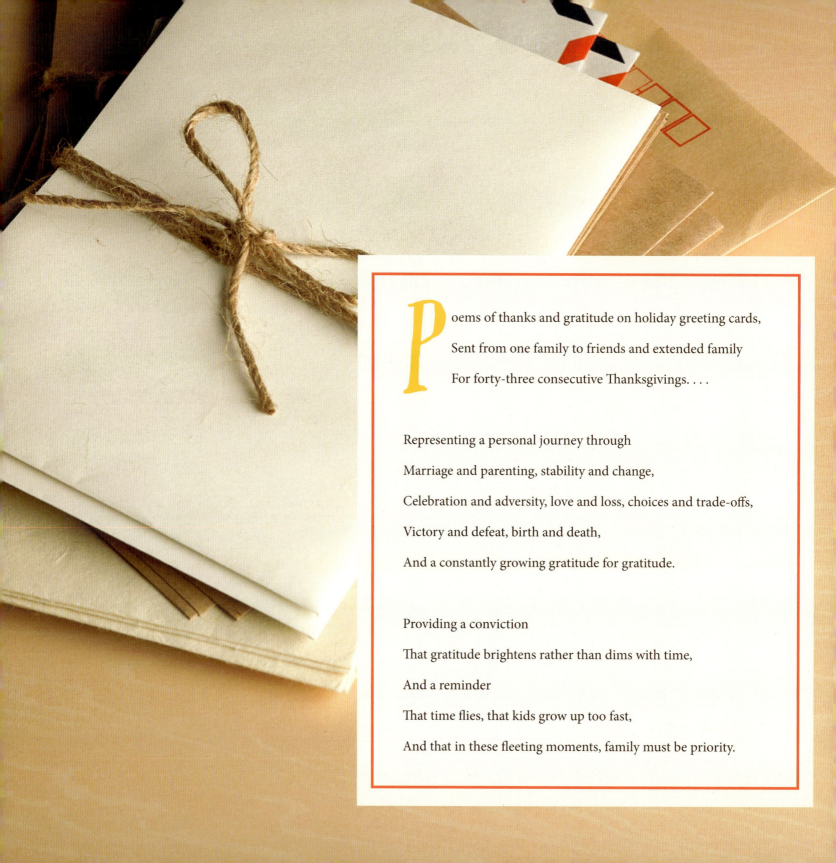

Poems of thanks and gratitude on holiday greeting cards,

Sent from one family to friends and extended family

For forty-three consecutive Thanksgivings. . . .

Representing a personal journey through

Marriage and parenting, stability and change,

Celebration and adversity, love and loss, choices and trade-offs,

Victory and defeat, birth and death,

And a constantly growing gratitude for gratitude.

Providing a conviction

That gratitude brightens rather than dims with time,

And a reminder

That time flies, that kids grow up too fast,

And that in these fleeting moments, family must be priority.

PART THREE

ONE FAMILY'S JOURNEY THROUGH GRATITUDE

43 YEARS OF PERSONAL POEMS OF

THANKS-GIVING FROM 1972 TO 2014

Simple Thanksgiving

We give thanks on this day
for our family
and for each of our precious friends.

No other treasure parallels the value
of a true friendship
because relationships are the prime source
of eternal joy.

The contribution that you
and each other friend and family member
has made in our lives
cannot be measured or even contemplated.
We only know that we face each day
with greater confidence
knowing that your love and loyalty sustains us.

We are deeply grateful to a loving Heavenly Father
Who has brought you into our lives,
and us into yours.
May He be as generous to you
and to those dear to you
as He has been to . . .

Rick and Linda Eyre and girls

*First two children . . . living and working in our first
job after graduate school, founding a political and
management consulting firm in Washington, DC.*

Two parents and two kids—all even, but not for long.

Relationships

Our thanks-giving on this special day
is for you . . .
because among God's many blessings,
it is our relationships with family and friends
that endure, fulfill, and form the substance
of which joy is made.
Indeed, a life void of all relationships
would have nothing left . . .
(except the potential
to create new relationships).

Our thanks-giving is to you
because
the touching
of your life and ours
has made our hearts smile,
and taught us the strength and confidence
that comes from loving and from being loved.

May the year ahead, for you, be one of
goals accomplished . . . and of serendipity
(happy surprises, unexpected joys).

Richard, Linda, Saren, Shawni, and ?

1973

Six of us now, and living in the Autumn Rocky Mountains.

Thanks-Giving for Joy

We have always felt glad
> that Thanksgiving precedes Christmas,
because in life, gratitude precedes joy.

Each year, in our family, it seems that joy expands
in proportion to the many things
> for which we give thanks.

In this world, and particularly in this season,
the branches and boughs of experience
are so often heavy with the blossoms of happiness,
and yet we know that the roots of joy are family and friends.

And so, on this special day,
> for what you have given us,
and for what He has given us,
we give thanks,
and love,
and joy.

Love, the Eyres

Late Autumn Transitions

late autumn's transitions:
leaves to bare limbs,
grass to snow,
the external warm of summer just passed
to the internal warm of Christmas just ahead . . .

also a transition of time . . .
a year ends,
a short era concludes.
transitions are times of reflection and of plans . . .
of looking over-the-shoulder-back
and over-the-horizon-forward.

for us, today, the reflecting-back
yields the swelling joy of thanks-giving . . .
the bursting gratitude
for health, for gifts, for opportunities,
and most of all (after all) for friends and family . . .
for you who make up our world . . . you whose touch,
once felt by our lives,
can never really un-touch . . .
though both time and people move.

for us, today, the looking forward
is a prayer . . .
may God grant you a joyous holiday season
and a year of progress, contribution and love.
may He grant us the same . . . and a continued chance
to cross our lives with yours.

the eyres / richard, linda, saren, shawni, joshua, saydria

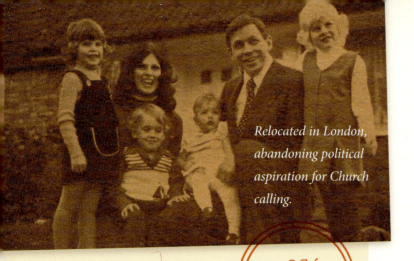

Relocated in London, abandoning political aspiration for Church calling.

British Thanksgiving

1976

We give thanks for life,
for joy,
for opportunities to serve, and for
the freedom-loving, God-fearing lands
of England and America.

People try to tell us that there is no
Thanksgiving day in Great Britain.
But there is . . .
Every day, in our hearts, for you,
our friends and family
who make life bright and warm,
sure and mellow.

Our hearts are in two places today . . .
Here, with those whom we serve,
and there, with you whom we miss,
and love.
May the Lord bless and keep you,
and may joy find you as frequently
as it finds the Eyres.

Family, Friends, and Missionaries

1977

family and friends are for sharing . . .
and for thanking . . .
and for sharing Thanksgiving and thanks-giving with.

this Thanksgiving we give thanks
to a wise and loving Heavenly Father
. . . . .   for a sensational new little son and for the miracles
              and blessings and growth that surrounded his birth,
. . . . .   for the joy and unfolding individuality
          of five precious children,
. . . . .   for 200 young missionaries who fit into our lives
          somewhere between brothers and sons,
sisters and daughters,
. . . . .   for the beauty and peace we feel in our lives,
. . . . .   and for having you to share it with.

this Thanksgiving we share with you the joy we feel . . .
through neck-level involvement in a worthy cause . . .
through learning and loving a new country so old . . .
through observing with a close-up lens
the positive alteration of lives . . .
through knowing you care and think of us once in a while.

love,

richard, linda, saren, shawni, josh, saydi, and new little jonah eyre

We give thanks . . . .

Seven of us now, becoming more British every day.

1978

Gratitude is Joy, Joy is Gratitude

Question:
Does "Joy" (the deepest happiness)
have many sources? . . . or only one?
You might think of many . . . but they might all boil down
(or at least relate)
to one.
And that one would be gratitude.
Gratitude is joy. Joy is gratitude. Thus Thanksgiving is the happiest time.

This Thanksgiving
we are strengthened by the squared scaffolding
of young missionaries who are stretched straight and pulled pure
by the challenge of working only for a cause.

The fact that this is our third of three British Thanksgivings
stirs and prickles our emotions . . . so that
      just as the pleasure of rejoining some loved ones comes close,
      the pain of leaving other, newer loves looms large
      and so we move up life's path . . . accepting both kinds of joy.

· Richard · Linda · Saren (8) · Shawni (6) · Joshua (4) · Saydi (3) ·
Jonah (1) and ? (Feb. 1979)

Thanks-Giving for Joy

Like Pilgrims,
from England to America we've come.

Like Pilgrims, thankful for the freedoms
and joys of this new country,
but missing mightily
the green and pleasant land behind.

Like Pilgrims, thankful
to a gracious God for a growing
family of children, whose presence
is peace,
whose light teaches joy.

Thankful to think of Him not just
as a force, a creator . . . but as a Father . . .
thus to think of you,
our most valued possessions,
not just as friends,
but as brothers, sisters.

Like Pilgrims, embarking on
new adventures,
secure in your friendship,
anxious for you to be secure in ours.

1979

Richard, Linda, Saren (9), Shawni (7),
Joshua (5), Saydi (4), Jonah (2), and
Talmadge (9 mo.).

The Harmony of the Harvest

Thanksgiving again . . .
so much the same, so much different.

We are thanks-giving
for the harmony of the harvest,
for the rhythms and cadences of life's rich experience,
for the alternating, peaceful strains
and dynamic crescendos of our young family,
including the new virtuoso soloist
who fills the room and makes us feel
more like a whole orchestra than mere chamber music.

. . . and for you, our family and friends,
so involved in the melodies of our life.
We are thanks-giving again, but it never grows old,
nor does our love for you, or your song's harmony with ours.

May the coming season, and the fresh new year to follow,
be filled with music, both for ear and soul . . .
life-music,
in-tune
with He who orchestrates all things,
with He to whom we give thanks.

The Eyres

Thanks to the Peaceable Author of Light

We give thanks!
For a higher realm that we are seeking and finding,
finding and seeking. . . .
A realm of light,
above the flesh and schemes and ruts of man,
A realm of truth and tears, flashes and fears,
Yearnings and years,
A realm we find in our quietest moments
surrounded with the soft sureness
that after the tumult and shouting dies, after the over-rated
successes and failures slide away,
it is you, our family and friends that matter, that continue,
and that go with freedom and faith as the 4 ingredients of joy.
We thank the peaceable author of light
whose spirit speaks its sweetest sermon to ours
in silent, simple moments when we wait.
He tells us then, that our love for you is love for Him . . .
and that
Thanksgiving is Joy.

THE EYRES, Richard, Linda, Saren (11), Shawni (9), Josh (7), Saydi (6), Jonah (4), Talmadge (2), & Noah (1)

Thanksgiving

I Love Autumn,
Not too hot, not too cold,
With all of beautiful leaves,
And <u>so</u> full of fun days.
There's Halloween, with Jack-o-lanterns,
Witches, and goblins.
Autumn is harvest time,
With all of the bright colored leaves.
But, the best part of Autumn is,
         Thanksgiving,
When we see our family,
All gathered together,
And relize how much each one means,
And give thanks to,
Our Heavenly Father

                    Saren Eyre age: 11
                    Oct. 28, 1981

Back to Washington with the Reagan administration.

1982

Families Unfold like Flowers

families unfold like flowers,
revealing new wonders, unexpected gifts
and diversity!
we give thanks for the new present, previously the future
which pushes now to then in its wake,
and wakes us
through the noise of growth and blossoming,
especially among our children.
and we give thanks for the constants among the change . . .
for the love and loyalty of family and friends . . .
for you!
thanksgiving signals the season of
free-flow feelings, warmth and joy,
but also melancholy, and memories,
some longings for other golden moments and for some of you,
too long away from our lives.
a little fear even, of the speed of time
and sadness in not being part of some of your changes.
but mostly, time carries new joy on its waves,
joy made of experience, challenge, surprise . . .
and of thanks-giving . . .
for a world where hope still outweighs hate,
for God-given knowledge of priorities, for the blessing
of "choosing the better part," and for
fellow travelers like you who share that choice
of faith and freedom, friends and families.
and through all the change and challenge, all the growth and gifts
the bottom line is
we love you!

The Eyres

The Harmony of the Harvest

For us,
Thanksgiving is a time to reflect
and realize. And "realize" or "real eyes," is a synonym
for Thanksgiving.

Our new year is not January but
September . . . the new school year.
And between its hustle and the Christmas bustle
comes a quieter moment,
in leafless November,
a time to look front and back,
to ponder and plan, to be grateful,
and to real eyes what matters.

The "desperate haste to succeed in
such desperate enterprises"
that Thoreau observed
has further fused in our day,
and we think too much in terms
of getting there, getting done, getting ahead,
getting . . .

and too little about the joy of the journey,
too little about real eyes ing.
In this scrambled, scrambling,
left-brain world, our eyes see the worries,
the ambitions and the tasks of the day.
But we have other eyes!
And when they see, what they see
is more real than the illusions on our retina.

At Thanksgiving, we try to see with
real eyes . . . to realize the awe of
A new baby . . . realize the joy of giving and serving
. . . realize the love we feel for you,
for family and friends, and for God
who gave you to us.
Such are the real eyes of Thanksgiving!

The Eye-ers: Linda, Richard, Saren, Shawni, Josh, Saydi,
Jonah, Talmadge, Noah, and Eli

1983

Birth of our last son and continued
moves back and forth between Salt
Lake City and Washington, DC.

Books Pass through Our Lives

1984

Books pass through our lives,
leaving traces, impressions, bringing to us the
perspectives of other people,
other places, other pastimes.

But more important than the books passing through our lives
are the lives that pass through our book.
People enter the book of our family
and move amongst its pages,
making memories, leaving love,
extending experience, enlarging expectations,
even expanding excitement.

You,
our family and friends,
warm the chapters of our book,
shaping a story that would otherwise be
short and shallow.
As we turn through the seasons of our book,
writing the chapters of our lives,
we acknowledge God who gave us paper and quill
and who, by including you,
made it a book of Thanksgiving.

*Richard, Linda, Saren (14) Shawni (12) Joshua (10) Saydi (9) Jonah
(7) Talmadge (5) Noah (4) Eli (1) EYRE*

More travel, more speaking, and publishing our tenth book.

Thanksgiving, Lifebalance, and the Eyrealm

Driving through flurrying, fast-flying, yellow leaves,
low, late-Autumn sunshine slanting sideways
under higher clouds, slate colored and moving.
We stop, alone amidst the bright motion, top down
to catch the spinners and listen to the swirlers
and think while we watch it all change.

Thanksgivings come so often now,
and life's busyness is both blessing and bother.
We would trade away little that we pursue,
and no one that we love,
yet we long for more simple solitude
and we look for ways to balance the priorities of
children . . . career . . . church,
of service and self—
to balance outer ambition with inner submission
and to bring our doing and our getting
into harmony with our being.

We look, each of us in our own way, for a higher realm
which balances structure with spontaneity,
schedules with serendipity.
We look for this balance amidst the change
which is the only constant
other than the sustaining love we feel from you,
our family and friends.
And we realize, in glimpses that blow past like golden leaves,
that change is the Eyrealm
and that Lifebalance is love.

We wish we saw you more, that our minds could meet
on change and other joys,
but at least our Thanksgiving reaches out far toward you—
mending memories, dividing distances,
and shrinking separation into a temporary disorder
which can be partially put right simply by saying
we love you!

Eyrealm

1985

Shifting from Life Planning to Life Balance, building cabin in woods.

Wondrous Waves of Pure Gratitude

1986

Gratitude is a gift and an art
mastered by few.
We remember our Swedish immigrant Grandmother in whom
thanksgiving would well up
to teary overflow
each time she prayed.
Some said it was because the contrasts remained so vivid
between how little she had there
and how much she had here.
Gratitude's opposites (and the norm for most) are
"wanting more" and
"taking for granted."

It is said (and it is sad) that, to really live you must almost die
and occasionally
we have a close call, a near miss, a "scary almost"
and, for a moment, we are filled, overwhelmed, refreshed
by penetrating, wondrous waves of pure gratitude.
But the intensity and the joy of those feelings dim and diminish
as soon as life returns to numb normal.
How do we make Thanksgiving a verb in our lives
instead of a noun on our calendars?
How do we make the intensity of our gratitude for what we keep match
the intensity of the grief we feel for what we lose?
How do we take nothing for granted and take everything for gratitude?
How do we feel the joy now instead of looking back with melancholy
when it is gone?

Thanksgiving is a time to try
A time to count the blessings and even imagine
the grief we would feel with their loss.

So we share this gratitude,
And we ask Him
to sharpen it in our souls, to heat it and hone it in our hearts.

Richard, Linda, Saren, Shawni, Joshua, Saydi, Jonah,
Talmadge, Noah, Eli and (as of June 12) Charity Jade Eyre

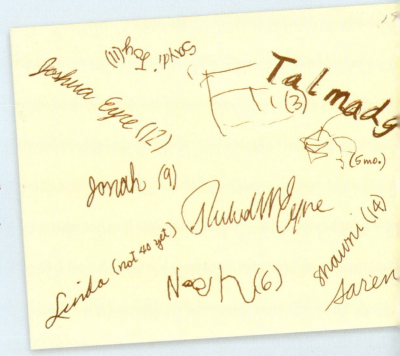

Our last daughter and last child arrives.
All nine at home.

Never Tack when You Can Jibe

Love: RICHARD, LINDA, SAREN (17) SHAWNI (15) JOSHUA (13) SAYDRIA (12) JONAH (10) TALMADGE (8) NOAH (7) ELI (4) CHARITY (1)
Not to mention Banner (the horse) Esmerelda (the dog) Geneva (the cat) Brumbie (the bird) Buba (the turtle) Cosette (the bunny) Bill (the gerbil)

1987

Some sailors say
"Never tack when you can jibe!"
Turn with the wind instead of into it . . . and
know thanksgiving for both breeze and sail.
Enjoy the force and power and ride the speed, cautious only
to keep control.

1987 was a year of joyous jibes for Eyrealm,
navigated in England,
where we wrote and watched, wandered and wondered
with the children,
reveling in their rediscovery of each other, and our rediscovery of our roots.
We focused on four ships that sailed
from Liverpool, Southampton, Stockholm, and Copenhagen,
bearing the bearers of the Eyre, Jacobson, Swenson, and Clark names—
the four corners of our family tree . . .
the four bearers who made right-angle jibes,
leaving the countries, cultures, and churches
of all past ancestral levels,
starting a new chapter—even a new book—for all of us who followed.

You and we are sailors on the same ship . . .
the category of people who make us what we are;
to whom we owe ourselves,
and for whom we feel a love too deep to be fully expressed.
For you, friends and family, for you who are us,
we give thanks,
and we pilot through life's forward jibes with you as the wind in our sails.

Another year in England with all nine to write and to look for roots.

1988

A sort of serendipity-of-spirit that makes
Interruptions interesting and turns obstacles into opportunities.
One also needs the unmoving islands of friends and family.

We give thanks
To the designer of this whole wonderfully random place and plan.
We give thanks for you!
We love this season of Thanks Giving which warms us
And points us toward the more sacred season
On a bridge called Gratitude
May we feel it deeply as we travel far.

Love,

Richard, Linda, Saren (Wellesley College), Shawni, Joshua, Saydi,
Jonah, Talmadge, Noah, Eli, Charity 2

Time Travel

Time travel,
Sounds fictional . . . yet takes on
Revved-up reality as we watch children grow,
And change, and move on to college.

Life somehow resembles a frantic, high-speed drive
In a crowded car . . .
Yet it's so much fun! Where would you rather be?
On the sidelines? Watching the race?
Sitting safe outside the screen?
Peering in at the dodgem cars colliding and people laughing?

No screen in real life, no boundaries, only endless
Uncertainty,
Which can be translated: "excitement."

In this trackless journey,
One needs a compass rather than a roadmap . . .

Stewardship

1989

Thanks giving for what?
Your new car? Your new job? Your new idea?
Your new talent? Your new cause? Your new baby?
A good list, for all are gifts.
A bad possessive personal pronoun, for none are yours.
Each is a gift of stewardship—
His because all is His,
Entrusted to us to use, to build, to enjoy, to share.

Our favorite holiday this, because thanks giving
Mirrors stewardship!
Thanks is given for the given,
Not for the earned because there is none of that.
Thanks giving implies acknowledging the source and
Gratitude to the Giver.

Why does it matter?
Simply because ownership roots grow branches of pride, envy,
Covetousness,
Competition, manipulation, greed, and stress;
While stewardship roots generate humility, gratitude,
Service, charity, guidance, and peace.

Our most joyful stewardship is you—friends and family.
You are given to us, and we give thanks.
Let us serve you, enjoy you, love you . . .
Even through means as small as this greeting.

Linda, Richard, Saren (19), Shawni (17), Joshua (15),
Saydria (14), Jonah (12), Talmadge (11), Noah (9), Elijah (6),
Charity (3)

Indian Summer

Decade changes shake us, awaken us, make us wonder
if we knew how happy we were—
those moments of birth, of beauty, of becoming—
Have we grasped them? Felt their full joy?
And now—are we fully reaching the present now?
We've tried, this round-year
through Kamakura summer and Winnepesaukee fall
to slow time and see now,
to appreciate '90 as we think about '00.

A life has seasons:
blooming vibrant spring,
full-heat summer, slower mellow fall, reflective winter.
What season, these '90s? Where are we?
Fort- something, completed family, some children leaving,
spinning off into their own orbits
(or twirling away like autumn leaves).

Summer seems past, yet we're not ready for fall.
So mentally we manage a fifth season—
Indian Summer,
still warmed by current children, present physical,
the fruit and seeds still ripening on our branch.
But fall forewarns—longer shadows,
sharper contracts of reality, crisper air.

Is it lower light or the best of two seasons combined?
The latter, because
even the more frequent frailties are a benefit.
Impressions of indestructibility give way
to aches and wheezes, surrender to reading glasses,
new consciousness of limitations and fragility.
We find ourselves admiring the smooth resilience
of youth—our children surpass us at what we just taught them.
Yet, we welcome it all, because we begin to see connections between
self-sufficiency and self-awareness.
As one slides, the other thins and we find ourselves
more humble, more grateful, more sensitive,
and more dependent on Him to whom
we give thanks
at this season.

Love, Richard, Linda, Saren (Wellesley College), Shawni (Boston
University), Josh, Saydi, Jonah, Talmadge, Noah, Eli, Charity

1990

Indian Summer

Decade changes shake us, awake us, make us wonder
If we knew how happy we were --
the moments of birth, of beauty, of becoming ...
Have we grasped them? Felt their full joy?
And now -- are we fully reaching the present now?
We've tried, this round-year,
through Kamakura summer and Winnepesaukee fall
to slow time and see now,
to appreciate 90 as we think about 00.

Out On a Limb

Secure, some seasons—soft and straight and stable—
nearly predictable from ease to ease.
Other times, though, we reach, struggle, climb . . . and go
out on a limb.
Pushed by purpose, coaxed by cause, we respond to restlessness
and depart the deft density and easy applause of the familiar
to teeter on a new life-branch
in higher, thinner air.

Our life's long, warm summer, of babies and bedtime stories,
of writing and touring and speaking, of "motherhood and apple pie"
yields to Indian summer.
Vivid, bright, but more biting, with
rough weather and the fate of fall everywhere near.
Part of our writing shifts with part of our thinking
from inside our home to outside—to schools, communities,
to our State and its future.

One thing to write about it, another to do about it.

We are always thankful for friends and family,
but more so now!
In this arena as surroundings and daily destinations grow less familiar,
the known, sure, stability of your support
steadies us.

And most, we give thanks
to Him who built all branches and lifts all limbs.
Who has given us the stewardship and the circumstance
and who had given us you.

Happy Thanksgiving 1991

EYREALM

Out On A Limb -- We Give Thanks!

(from left) Charity (5), Saren (21), Talmadge (12), Saydi (16), Eli (8), Jonah (14), Josh (17), Shawni (19), Noah (11), Linda, Richard

Visiting every town in Utah in preparation for gubernatorial race.

Working, Winning, Losing, Sharing

The Campaign.

Be "actively engaged" says scripture.

"That which does not kill us makes us stronger," said someone else.

Be "in the arena" said T. Roosevelt, and never "among those cold and timid souls
who never knew either victory or defeat."

Said Rudyard Kipling, "Meet with triumph and disaster,

And treat those two imposters just the same."

We knew victory in the Summer Convention and defeat in the Fall Election.

We worked hard . . . with the book, the ideas (now with a life of their own),

the board, the staff, countless citizens . . . the eleven of us Eyres,

in this emotional window of time.

Saren and Shawni back from Wellesley and Israel before Church missions.

Josh awaiting study abroad, the smaller ones giving their summer to the cause.

Imploding, density, intensity, together,

Clustered, compressed, channeled on a confined course . . .

Working, winning, losing, sharing.

Appropriate that this season of thanksgiving follows . . . mellow, vivid, still-warm

Time to reflect, realize, restructure. Time to feel gratitude, deep and still,

For you, dear family and friends, to you for loyalty and support

Well beyond our hopes and dreams.

Like moody weather or sudden storms, adversity and disappointment

Are gratitude-enhancers, deepening the tones and contrasts,

Awakening awareness of beauty, of people,

Of the sweeping current of this one particular time on earth

When we can get to anywhere, and everywhere is still different.

We're better for the attempt, and we love you more.

We tried to change a little part of the world

And ended up changing a little part of ourselves.

Happy Thanksgiving!

*Shawni (20, just called to Budapest, Hungary mission—will serve in Romania), Joshua
(18, leaving Jan. 12 for Jerusalem), Saydi (17, exploring colleges for next year), Saren
(22, just called to Sofia, Bulgaria Mission), Noah (12), Charity (6), Talmadge (13), Eli
(9), Linda, Richard, Jonah (15), insert, away when photo was taken)*

*A New York Times
#1 Bestseller; Back to
Washington and in
Israel.*

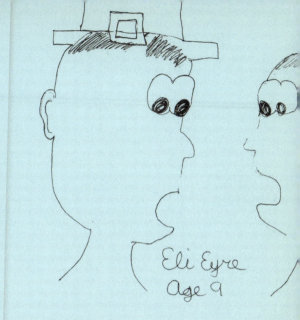

Eli Eyre
age 9

Blessings

Eastern autumn.
The feel of late fall—mellow, moist, mist-rising mornings,
Wet, leaf-covered paths through high, bright-colored woods,
Swirling yellow leaf showers in the gusts,
Halloween smell, slanting sunshine.

Blessings . . .
This year they have twirled down on us like someone shook the tree.
Books have sold, parents have rallied, causes have grown,
Missionaries have departed (three) and have been powerfully blessed,
Are they part of the blessings or the cause of them?

"Blessings" . . .
The connotation is one of gratitude and gifts,
Not earned or envied, not developed or deserved.
More than foolish—impossible—to take credit
For Gifts too great even to comprehend,
Let alone to survey or summon self-satisfaction.

Blessings . . .
The vast freedom, the boundless opportunity of living now.
The wonder of brothers and sisters who became our children and
Now are becoming our (and each other's) teachers and examples.
An orphanage in the Transylvanian Alps, a #1 national best seller,
A son returning to our old mission in London, and us
Returning for a respite to our first home in Virginia.

Blessings, twirling down like someone shook the tree.
None brighter than you, friends and family. . . .

We give thanks!

Richard & Linda, McLean; Saren (23), Bulgaria; Shawni (21)
Romania; Josh (19), London; Saydi (18), Wellesley College; Jonah
(16), Talmadge (14), Noah (12), Eli (10), Charity (7).

The Final Question

Gratitude, Appreciation, Thanksgiving: are these
expressions? emotions? attitudes?
qualities of the spirit?
are they also an art . . . a skill . . .
an awareness / aptitude / ability
that can be discovered, developed?
if an art, then an art worth working on
because these are both the manifestations and the prompters
of real happiness.
blessings are the seeds of our joy.
gratitude is not only the cultivation but the harvest.
writing this card is a chance each year
to practice the art.
then we send it to you—family and friends
other subjects of our thanksgiving:
living now (earth's most commotional, creative, culminating moment).
cause embodied as career (we write and speak on values, balance, families
and in optimistic moments feel society moving that way).
reversing roles with children as they become our teachers
(we sense that they are bigger and better spirits than we)
two missionary daughters (home from eastern europe)
and joined by a third daughter as a troika of college roommates.
a son still serving in England
(and another who faced down death and came out stronger).
twenty-five years of a partnership (that is still getting better).
having finally overcome the political bug that bit us.
even turning fifty (for one who thinks he'll be 100,
the half-way peak is highest—
offering widest panorama, perspective, paradigm).
the final question about thanks-giving
(after we know it and its subjects)
is its recipient (who do we give it to?)
one answer is you.

but the real answer (and our thanksgiving testimony)
is God, our Heavenly Father,
whose hand we acknowledge in all things
and whose blessings we pray upon you.

Eyrealm

By Charity (8)

Indian Meets Pilgrim
And Turkey Meets
His DOOM!

*Thirtieth book, more
missionaries, three
college-roommate
daughters.*

"We Give Thanks . . ."

Awakening a Trivialized Word

1995

"Gratitude"
A trivialized word, or at least undervalued.
We say "thanks"—or feel a fleeting wave
of appreciation—just a thin skin
covering over our take-for-granted mantra mentality.

Instead, gratitude can be a joyful awakening to God's glory,
to our own dependent childhood,
our ultimate-potential nothingness,
a powerful spiritual emotion,
thrilling us to our core, tearing our eye,
striking deep-space awe
and humility so pure it hurts.

Without humility we develop a preposterous paradigm
of world-shrinking, self-bloating arrogance
or imagined self-sufficiency.
Humility has only two approaches:
crisis or gratitude.
And scripture calls "more blessed" those who are
"humble without being compelled to be humble" (approach two).

Not some luxury then, gratitude,
not some diversion to indulge in occasionally,
not mere etiquette or brief warmth-flashes.
But a way of life, a profound gift/skill
itself worthy of high thanks
involving seeing, feeling, sharing, and abundant love,
yielding humility, perspective, peace, and abundant joy.

We feel it deeply now, this season, for you.

Eyrealm: First row, David (25) and Shawni (23) Pothier, Charity (9), Saren (25),
Eli (12), Josh (21), Linda. Back row: Talmadge (16), Saydi (20), Noah (15), Jonah
(18), Richard

We Give Thanks

a powerful spiritual emot
thrilling us to our core, te
striking deep-space awe
and humility so pure it hu

Without humility we deve
of world-shrinking, self-bl
or imagined self-sufficienc
Humility has only two app
crisis or gratitude.
And scripture calls "more b
"humble without being com

Not some luxury then, grati
not some diversion to indulg
not mere etiquette or brief w
But a way of life, a profoun
(itself worthy of high thank
involving seeing, feeling, sha
yielding humility, perspective

We feel it deeply now, this se

Fourth and fifth missionaries, and a new trio of books.

Serendipity, Stewardship & Synergicity

At a time when so many seek control,
we give thanks for our lack of it.
For surprise, for the unexpected,
for the adventure of each new remarkably unpredictable day,
for the humility that tells us how little we really control,
for spiritual serendipity . . .
the awareness and the guidance that lets us try
to find something good while seeking something else,
to be a small part of God's plan instead of a large part of our own,
to cross the bridge between our goal and His will.

At a time when so many seek ownership,
we give thanks for our lack of it.
For the sure knowledge that all is God's,
for the awe and the wonder of using all He has entrusted,
for spiritual stewardship . . .
that erases both jealousy and pride
and reminds us of the glorious everythingness of His Fatherhood
and the joyful nothingness and endless potential of our childhood.

At a time when so many seek independence
we give thanks for our lack of it.
For our interconnectedness and mutual dependency,
for you—our family and friends—without which
we would have nothing—and be nothing,
for spiritual synergicity . . .
the magic of a whole greater than the sum of its parts—etched with divine timing,
body and spirit, spouse with spouse, friend to friend, man and God.

Richard, Linda, Saren at Harvard, Shawni and Dave Pothier in DC, Josh at BYU,
Saydi in Madrid, Jonah in London, Talmadge (17), Noah (16), Eli (13), Charity (10)
at home

Representing the New Generation

Sure . . .
We could have sent
the usual family picture
Except that Saydi is in Madrid
and Jonah is in London
and besides,
Max is the man to see!
Grandchild number ONE,
pride of five Eyre uncles
and three Eyre aunts,
the perfect combination of Shawni and Dave,
and the start
of a whole new generation of blessings.

We watch the tumultuous transition
from our high perspective
just over the crest of life's midpoint.
The way down (ahead) is not nearly as steep
as the way up (behind).
In fact, it's so gradual we notice no decline at all.
Just easier speed, less resistance.
The clear, joyful awareness of coasting.

Ten times as much in the second half . . .
due to the ease and speed
of the long, smooth incline,
and to accumulated access, assets, abilities,
and to the simple fact
that we can see more from up here.

So we go down gradually . . .
but we extend out dramatically!

What a deal!
What a time!
And grand kids too!
And friends like you!
WE GIVE THANKS!

Love, Eyrealm

First grandchild, high school basketball, crammed kids' schedules.

Be happy to the MAX!

Waning and Waxing

We Give Thanks
for a Growing Family Tree (see other side)

Time flight! Fear of flying or joy in passage?
Both. And, pondering them, a heightened awareness
Of the waxing and waning within our lives.

Waning: Inhabitants of the house
        Diapers and dishes, laundry and loose ends
        Music lessons and homework sessions
        Scouting and shouting
        Saturday baths and helping with math.

Waxing: Long-distance calls and long-distance flights
        Missions and marriages
        Graduations and big occasions
        E-mailing and sailing, candle lighting and check writing
        College admissions and current-year additions
        (a grand daughter, a son-in-law, a TV show, a book).

Along with these mandatory movements of maturity
Come the optional opportunities.
And we opt for:
Less quantity, more quality, less scrambling, more service.
Less hurry and hassle, more humor and harmony.
Less ire, more Eye-er.
Less future focus, more present and past pondering.
Less prose and pace, more poetry and peace.
Less Halloween and more Thanksgiving.
Less getting and more and more and more gratitude
to you and for you—family and friends.

Love, EYREALM

1998

Speaking engagements and
TV shows, as kids scatter.

Of the waxing and waning within our li
Waning: Inhabitants of the house
           Diapers and dishes, laundry a
           Music lessons and homework
           Scouting and shouting
           Saturday baths and helping wi
Waxing: Long-distance calls and long-di
           Missions and marriages
           Graduations and big occasions
           E-mailing and sailing, candle li
           College admissions and current

Millennium: Better and Better

So fortunate are we
Who divide our lives between two millennia.
We live at the dramatic apex where history meets future.
The best of both,
The exotic diversity of before's undiluted cultures
And the instant access of after's infinite connections.
The only generation that can go in hours by plane
Or seconds by Internet,
To places without McDonalds or white faces
(Mwambalazi, Kenya, and Tuni, Bolivia).

We partake of
All the pleasant possibilities of this last, peaceful pause
Before the culminating crescendo.

Here, now, in that moderated measure,
There is such pleasure.
We live and work in an extended Indian summer,
Wondering under the perfect sky how it can keep getting better
And better.
Nature itself becomes deeper and richer.
Or is it our capacity to enjoy?
Our vertical children become our horizontal friends
And the parents of our spectacular grandchildren.
We are more present in our passions,
More feeling, more moved by art or sport,
Thinking and writing ripples toward greater clarity,
And the Gospel becomes ever warmer, richer, more relevant.

The only appropriate response is Thanksgiving . . .
For when we live,
As well as where, and how, and with whom.
Another Thanksgiving. Last of this Millennium. Better and better.

WE GIVE THANKS

1999

Two married, two grandkids, humanitarian work in Africa and Bolivia.

Eyres: Richard, Linda, Eli and Charity (SLC); Saren and Jared and ? (SF); Dave and Shawni, Max and Elle (VA); Josh (DC), Saydi (NYC), Jonah (Boston), Talmadge (Brazil), Noah (Hawaii)

Then, Now, and Forever

2000

Twenty people and a dog in this photo now,
Twenty people!
Time slips, slides, shifts, and sifts away like sand blowing.
Leaving, as it clears, numbers that increase geometrically.
With generations and geometry working for us, the faces
On each year's card get smaller and more numerous.
We start imagining something akin to nine times nine times nine.
Branches thrust out through the sky
Into eternity. Life after, kingdoms beyond.
In that direction of hope,
Family is the expanding joy of births, marriages, and grandchildren.

But for Thanksgiving perspective, turn your glance away
from the branches and sight down along the trunk.

Break the surface barrier and tunnel the roots—
down through the entire earth and out
Into the other side of eternity, life before, Kingdom past.
In that direction of worth, family is God,
and you were brother or sister,
Waiting with us for a turn in mortality

The dynamic present draws its joy from both directions. . . .
So at Eyrealm we lived this year writing about and balancing our
Past and future paradigms.
Backward and forward eternities—one continuum making us
Eternally grateful for you,
Friends and family,
Then, now, and forever

Rick and Linda; Saren; Jared and Ashton (San Jose); Shawni, Dave, Max, and Elle (McLean, VA); Josh (Washington DC); Saydi (Columbia, NYC): Jonah and Aja (Harvard, Cambridge); Talmadge (SLCC); Noah (Santiago, Chile); Eli; Charity (East High); and Able (dog house).

...me slips, slides, shifts and sifts away like
Leaving, as it clears, numbers that increas
With generations and geometry working for
on each year's card get smaller and more
We start imagining something akin to nine
Branches thrust out through the sky
into eternity, life after, kingdoms beyond.
In that direction of *hope*,
family is the expanding joy of births, marria
grandchildren.

But, for Thanksgiving perspective,
turn your glance away from the branches a
sight down along the trunk.

Break the surface barrier and
tunnel the roots – down through the entire e
into the other side of eternity, life before, kin
In that direction of *worth*,
family is God, and you were brother or siste
waiting with us for a turn in mortality.

The dynamic present draws its joy from both
so at Eyrealm we lived this year writing abou
past and future paradigms.
Backward and forward eternities – one conti
eternally grateful for you

Six Graduations

A Harvest!
Six graduations in the spring
(Eli, Tal, Aja, Saydi, Adam, and Courtney)
Three new grandchildren in the summer
(Grace, Isaac, and Aniston).

And so long a history of Thanksgiving Cards. This is number Thirty.
Other years we would pick some random theme of personal interest
For our poem—what an unappreciated luxury that was.
This fall that casual choice was obliterated
By a titanic terrorist tragedy,
Media magnified to gargantuan proportions.
Numbing body, mind and heart—but not soul!
For this is an old story of secret vs. sunlight,
And we trust all to Him.

It serves to remind us of the ongoing fact of our total vulnerability,
Exposing the lying illusions
Of control, independence, and ownership,
And opening us to the beauty and reality of their three counterpoint truths:
The serendipity of our need for God's guidance
    And the pleasure of watching for His will;
The synchronicity of our dependence on Him
    And our interdependence on each other;
And the stewardship of acknowledging our nothingness
    And His everythingness.

"...Live in thanksgiving daily..." (alma 34:38)

Thirtieth card, and a year with six graduations, six grandkids, and a regular segment on Good Morning America.

Within these three realities
Is a place of perfect priorities and peace
That engulfs us and reminds us that it is you—
Our friends and family—who matter,
And who always will.

Eyrealm

Miracles and Full Nesters

Another year: An emptier nest and writing about it.
Misnomer though—
Its fuller than ever before, full of memories but also
    Full of evolving, expanding family challenges,
    Full of drop-by entourages of college sons
    and high school daughter,

And often full of four Eyrealm generations
at event-prompted reunions. . . .
    Blessings, Births, Baptisms, Ballgames, Birthdays,
    Anniversaries, Graduations, Performances, Farewells,
    Weddings, Homecomings, Holidays.

The old nest has morphed from practice court to game-day arena,
A venue for big events.
Forget that conjured image of a brittle, stinky empty nest,
    Dried up, stark, prickly, and ready to crumble into dust.

The worn old nest buds out again—a perennial!
All the nourishing that happened here germinates and
Breathes life back into the twigs and they begin to flower.

A new flightling takes a living branch and transplants it.
Second generation nests begin to appear afar.

We feel less like a nest shrinking than like a garden growing.
More like a spring than a fall.

The revitalized mother nest goes mobile:
Bear Lake, Jackson, or Kolob.
A moving target for return migrators.

Miracles: Nests that fly, sticks with buds, roots with wings,
Children who teach their parents, and
Places on the earth that become places in the heart.

Our nest runneth over!

Thanks Giving to you and for you friends
and family who furnished
Some of our twigs, now woven forever
Into our hearts.

Eyrealm

2002

*Fourth wedding,
eighth missionary,
fortieth book,
heads spinning.*

Turn the Hearts, Repair the Breach

2003

Two ancient prophets who saw our day and
Offered their three-word solutions:

Malachi saw materialism and the mayhem of misplaced priorities
And warned on the last page of the Old Testament, of a whole world wasted
Unless, within families, we would
"Turn our Hearts."

Isaiah in his 58th chapter, saw an earth divided, a growing gap
Between rich and poor,
Two sides both suffering,
One from starving scarcity and one from selfish surplus.
He challenged us to
"Repair the Breach."

Both prophets' solutions are two-edged swords that swing both ways,
Parents' hearts turning to children, children's hearts to parents,
Rich's resources curing poor as poor's perspectives cure rich.

Both fixes have a macro and micro:
Heart-turning is a political fix for society and a personal fix for families.
Breach-repair can stop wars in the world and hubris in the home.

Both solutions can turn the two most common objects
of passive Thanks-giving: Family and Posterity
Into the two most powerful subjects of active Thanks-giving:
Nurturing and Charity

*Love, from Saren and Jared +3 in San Jose, Shawni and Dave +4 and Josh
in Phoenix, Saydi and Jeff in Cambridge, Jonah and Aja +2 in Auckland,
NZ, Talmadge in SoCal, Noah in Provo, Eli in Tokyo, Charity in Salt Lake,
Grandma Ruthie in Logan, Eva and Adam +1 in San Diego, Eldar and
Courtney in Provo, Rick and Linda on a plane*

Repairing the Breach

Thanksgiving, Family, and the Second Half

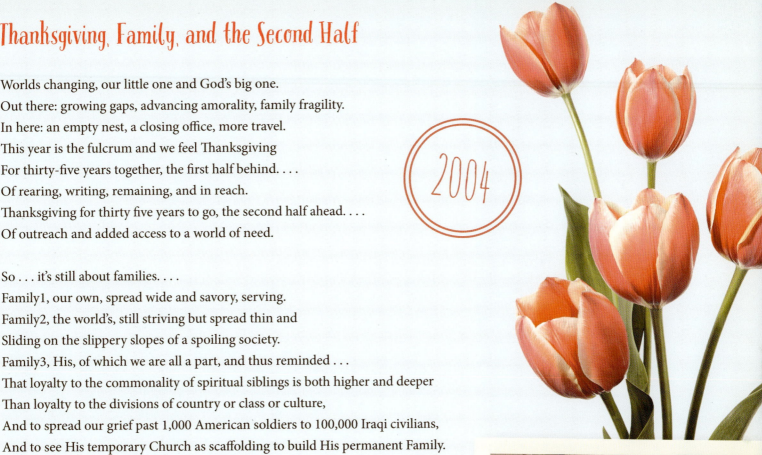

Worlds changing, our little one and God's big one.

Out there: growing gaps, advancing amorality, family fragility.

In here: an empty nest, a closing office, more travel.

This year is the fulcrum and we feel Thanksgiving

For thirty-five years together, the first half behind. . . .

Of rearing, writing, remaining, and in reach.

Thanksgiving for thirty five years to go, the second half ahead. . . .

Of outreach and added access to a world of need.

2004

So . . . it's still about families. . . .

Family1, our own, spread wide and savory, serving.

Family2, the world's, still striving but spread thin and

Sliding on the slippery slopes of a spoiling society.

Family3, His, of which we are all a part, and thus reminded . . .

That loyalty to the commonality of spiritual siblings is both higher and deeper

Than loyalty to the divisions of country or class or culture,

And to spread our grief past 1,000 American soldiers to 100,000 Iraqi civilians,

And to see His temporary Church as scaffolding to build His permanent Family.

It's hopeful and heartening

To bounce around the world, each landing vastly different

In cultural, ethnic, racial, religious, political, and economic trappings,

But similar and synonymous in the feelings, the hopes, and the love

Parents feel for their children.

But it's horrific and heart rending

To see family, the basic block of which society and eternity are built,

Ebbing, eroding, sometimes exploding in the death beam

Focused by the fracturer who knows broken bricks topple the whole building.

How to enlist freedom, fortune, and all of us

From Family1 in the service of Family2 and the cause of Family3?

We start with a mission statement for the second half:

"FORTIFY FAMILY: Celebrate Commitment, Popularize Parenting, Validate Values, Bolster Balance"

EYREALM

Bali and near full-time travel, online card, Family Vision Statement.

Where does Gratitude lead?

Thanks giving, the art, requires a subject as well as an object.
It must be to someone as well as for something.

An atheist's "to" is limited to circumstance and other people.
Gratitude to God is vastly wider and endlessly deep.

At its bright surface, like sun sparkling on the ocean, it is for
the simple satisfaction of a good day,
the beauty of a sunset,
the relief of a safe trip,
the pleasure in a child's accomplishment.
But beneath, its currents of emotion pull us to tears, to faith, and to genuine joy.
Deep for relationships,
Deeper for opulent options and opportunities,
Deeper still for purpose and mercy,
And finally to depths beyond what we can see for the family enveloping eternity
That divine thanks giving encompasses.

Where does gratitude lead? True gratitude?
To entitlement notions of privilege and pride?
To take-for-granted feelings and expectations of excess?
To sedentary satisfaction?
Or does true thanks giving trigger destiny, duty, and the desire to repay?

If you think "the latter"
Then you will understand, and perhaps join in some fashion,
Our cause to strengthen families,
Which we believe is the one way to save the world.

Love, EYREALM

We Give Thanks...

Two Ways to Live, and Think, and Thank

2006

for family...

Living, Type A

Be proactive, be in charge,
Be self confident,
Take control of your life.
Depend on yourself and go get things.
Act, don't react.
Plan your work, then work your plan.
Only you can know what you want,
And only you can decide your life.
Set your goals, make your plans,
and let no one stand in your way.

Cultivate strength and knowledge,
Which separates man and Maker.

View your life as a series of competitions,
And as an ongoing effort to prove yourself,
And rise above your rivals.

Understand that achievements
Are life's measure,
And wrap your identity
in positions and possessions.

Let the "W&P" phrases be your guide:
Work and Plan
Will and Purpose
Winning and Pride
Worry and Pursuit
Wealth and Power

Living, Type B

Be spiritually active,
Seek guidance, be humble,
Turn your life over to God,
And depend on Him.
Strive to understand His plan
And seek His will,
For only He knows what is best
For your eternal Soul.
Be aware of His nudges and impressions,
Notice the needs of those around you,
And don't win at others' loss.

Cultivate awareness and perspective.
(The differences between man and Maker).

View your life as a series of opportunities
to serve, and an adventure in discovering
Who God wants you to be.

Know that relationships are life's measure,
And wrap your identity in your family.

Model your life after W&P words:
Watch and Pray
Wander and Ponder
Wonder and Probe
Worship and Praise
Waken and Perceive
Wait and Procrastinate (selectively)
Width and Perspective
Wisdom and Peace

Love, EYREALM

Is it a Noun, Verb, or Adjective?

"Thanks-Giving" . . . Is it a Noun? (holiday/season/long weekend)

Or a Verb? (appreciation/acknowledgment/attitude of heart)

Or an Adjective? (describing the kind of persons we long most to be)

Perhaps . . .

The noun is there to prompt us to practice the verb,

So that we might one day wear the well-fitting adjective.

To this end, this year,

As a TG(noun) greeting, we send you

Our A-list workout regimen for TG(verb):

Ask for and develop the

Appreciation for life and the

Awareness of small connections that

Allows us to thank the

Author of every blessing every day.

Add the remarkable

Attitude of Serendipity, Stewardship, and Synergicity* and

Adopt the spiritual perspective of

Awe, thus cultivating our

Ability to receive with grace and to gradually

Acquire the joy-giving, joy-gaining

Art of

Acknowledging His hand in

All things. Then, daily,

Ascribe to Him as you Inscribe your journal.

Sending this TG(adj.) greeting,

To you and for you.

*With Love, from the great, full, thanks-giving Eyrealm: Linda and
Rickey (SLC), Saren and Jared +5 (SGU), Shawni and Dave +5
(PHX), Josh (PHX), Saydi and Jeff +2 (BOS), Jonah and Aja +3
(SGU), Talmadge (JFK), Noah and Kristi +1 (JFK), Eli (SLC), Charity
(BOS until Christmas, then as missionary, LHR)*

2007

What it is

The first thing to do when you wake,
The last thing to do before sleep,
The beginning of every prayer,
The end of every blessing,
The magnet of spirit,
The entry to solace,
The portal to peace.

THANKSGIVING

The prerequisite of perspective,
The acquisition of awareness,
The residue of responsibility,
The essence of experience,
The wonder of all our wonderings,
The fondness of friends,
The foundation of family.

THANKSGIVING

The deepest of holidays,
The purest of motives,
The sweetest of desires,
The surest of faiths,
The presence of God,
The core part of love.

Love, EYREALM

Informing on Thanks-Giving

Thanksgiving is about seeing and sharing blessings.
We believe the best blessings are beliefs,
So let us forward a score of our fondest to you in the form of forms,
And in a format that tries, humbly, to raise the common denominator
Enough to perhaps, in the mind at least, re-form reality.

Because sometimes, in the mode of thanks-giving,
We are lifted out of the material world
Toward a higher awareness, a broader perspective,
Wherein. . . .

> Our form of success is relationships,
> Our form of independence is interdependence,
> Our form of control is serendipity,
> Our form of recreation is re-creation,
> Our form of ownership is stewardship,
> Our form of leadership is service,
> Our form of self-help is personal inspiration and guidance,
> Our form of confidence is faith,
> Our form of marriage is eternal commitment,
> Our form of déjà vu is a pre mortal life,
> Our form of freedom is agency and truth,
> Our form of children is brothers and sisters,
> Our form of God is Father,
> Our form of family is an envelope within God's family,
> Our form of service and giving is consecration,
> Our form of meditation is prayer,
> Our form of death is birth,
> Our form of ultimate source is living prophets,
> Our form of peace is the Holy Spirit,

And finally wherein our form of wealth is friends,
Among which we count you, and wish you, with love,
Happy Thanksgiving, 2009, from the Eyrealm.

Thanks-Giving and Receiving

days shorten, skies darken, snow is in the air,
thoughts turn to gathering and gifting
in today's world, which honors proactive controlling and competing . . .
is there room for receiving?

in a paradigm where a Heavenly Father has all, and wants to give us all,
which is the greater gift, the topmost talent, the supreme skill—
the ability to achieve, accomplish, and acquire?
or the reverence to receive?

does "receive" have to be a re-active, passive word?
or can it be a vibrant verb—
a light-filled challenge—an art and a gift?
can it be the perfect complement to the generosity of God?

a perfectly thrown pass or a perfectly given gift counts nothing
if it is dropped
the receiver completes the quarterback and gets passed to more often
blessings multiply, joy abounds

giving and receiving are not opposites, but two sides
of one spinning, sparkling coin
the receiver gives the appreciation that empowers the giver
the giver receives the gratitude that rewards the receiver

our three, year-ending holidays form an interesting sequence
the dark ghouls of Halloween are transformed
into the light angels of Christmas
by the redeeming recognition of receiving
we call it Thanks-Giving—
the middle, transitional holiday that lifts us from dark to light

From Eyrealm: Saren and Jared +5 in UT, Shawni and Dave + 5 and Josh in PHX, Saydi and Jeff + almost 4 in BOS, Jonah and Aja + almost 4 in SEA, Talmadge and Anita in NYC, Noah and Kristi +3 in the OC, Eli and Julie in DC, Charity in SFO, and us empty nesters in SLC and on airplanes.

The Richness of Autumn

Juxtaposition of cool air in my nostrils and hot sun on the back
Slanting, revealing light, deeper shadows, flaming foliage
Some mornings surprising with snow skiff or frost

Autumn, always the favorite season
And now the season of our lives
Our axis tilts slowly, and stretches our mortal year across nine seasons

A long, growing spring through school and mission and marriage
An early summer of new babies and politics and another mission
A midsummer with full-bloom cacophony of conceived children and books
The lush late summer's missions and marriages and Jerusalem study abroad
Indian summer of central three-campus kingdom and orbiting satellites
And now full autumn, rich and boundless
Then fall, more as a mellow invitation than a lowering threat
Followed by early winter's renewed energy and new snow
And finally the reflective soft silence and reward of deep winter

We love this sixth season because it is now, the last third of the second third
Late enough for perspective but early enough for energy
Bright leaves, some flying in the wind and some still on the tree
We are the eye-ers or seers into the eyes of our nine noble ones
Family members 40 and 41 set to enter this estate as grandchildren 22 and 23
We float on new volumes and audiences to the domains of daughters and sons
Wrapped in each other's oneness, flying far and then homing again and again
To the warmth of three campuses that become physical legacy
Fresh books on entitlement and spiritual solutions
A little early snow from a surgery shoulder and a bungled back previews winter
and enhances returning equine and athletic appreciation

Abundance abounds and giving lags receiving so we get constantly and gratefully more behind
Only our ever-indebted liabilities can balance His ever-given assets
Our thanks-giving forms in the mold of our inability ever to repay

Eyrealm

2011

Half travel,
half home, 100
countries visited .

Giving Thanks for Three Places

This Thanksgiving we divide our
Thanks-Giving twice into three parts,
first by place and then by time. . . .

Giving thanks for three places:
The Outer of opportunity and contribution,
The Inner of family and relationships,
The Inner-inner of testimony and peace,
And finding that these three gratitudes help
balance priorities and perspectives.

Then, seeking yet another way to feel, giving thanks for three times:
The mellow stewardship of past memories,
The moving serendipity of present moments,
The marvelous synergicity of future milestones,
And discovering that each of these three thanks equates to joy.

Both threes, in place and in time, funnel down to you,
family and friends—
Center of our heart, heart of our thanksgiving.

With love, from Eyrealm
An Eye-er sees, and a realm is a tiny envelope
within His vast one,
Within which we humbly evolve from gratitude to generosity
And pass torches like batons, knowing that it is family
That will lead us back to Him.

THANKS Eyrealm

Starting EyresFreeBooks.com and continuing TheEyres.com.

2012

Takeforgranted vs. Thanksgiving

I glanced at Linda, holding a baby grandchild,
And saw her as an angel of light.
At times, unbidden, other brief glimpses come—
Of earth, of family, of my own body,
Supernal little knowings, suffused with pure perspective,
And generating a flash of unspeakable gratitude and clarity.

These glimpses accuse and convict us of our less-aware usual state, and
Of the universal, tragic, human sin of takeforgranted—
Getting used to glory—to the point where we don't see it anymore,
Don't feel it.
Desensitized to the Divine.

"All that is necessary for the triumph of evil," said Burke,
"Is for good men to do nothing."
A corollary:
"All that is necessary for the victory of flat, takeforgranted boredom,
Is for passion and striving and deep-feeling to drag and diminish."

Excess technology and endless data dumb us down from art and excellence;
Routine and plenty rob us of mind-stretching challenge;
Concrete and convenience pave over rugged, real nature.

Can we keep all of the new and the now,
But learn to juxtaposition it with what it threatens to replace?

Gratitude, the Joy Catalyst,
Is constantly challenged by takeforgranted,
Which shoves down and submerges awareness and appreciation
Holding them under where they can't breathe, beneath the dull weight
Of ease and entitlement.

At Thanksgiving, can we swim back up into consciously thankful joy?

2013

*All adult Eyrealm members at
Grandma Ruthie's funeral.*

HAPPY THANKSGIVNG

*Rick and Linda, Saren and Jared +5 in Utah,
Shawni and Dave +5 and Josh in Arizona,
Saydi and Jeff +4 in Boston, Jonah and Aja
+5 in Hawaii, Tal and Anita +1 and Eli and
Julie +1 in NYC, Noah and Kristi +5 in SoCal,
Charity in Palo Alto, and all of us deep within
our gratitude for you!*

Sometimes holiday greeting cards from parents,
And the family letters that accompany them,
Are all about their children's accomplishments.
And why not!?
They are fruits in a way, fruits of a nurtured tree.

None of us are perfect, and none have perfect kids,
But Thanksgiving and Christmas are times to emphasize the positive,
So here we are, indulging, bragging about some of the
Contributions our grown children are currently
Making to un-grown children, and to formative families
(Grabbing our family-focused baton, improving on it, and making it their own).

SAREN, co-founder of Powerofmoms.com,
benefiting hundreds of thousands of deliberate moms throughout the world
SHAWNI, author of an extraordinary mommy blog, 71toes.blogspot.com,
and named National Young Mother of the year by the American Mothers Org.
JOSH, wildly popular third grade teacher influencing hundreds of children
And creating balance and values-centered curriculums
SAYDI, creative professional family photographer
and volunteer one-on-one social worker
JONAH, entrepreneur and creative thinker,
inspiring others to a more economic and natural lifestyle,
TALMADGE, Instituting Imagine Learning, an online English language program
In NYC and getting a Master's degree from UPenn,
NOAH, a manager for Imagine Learning in California,
working on his MBA at USC
ELI, Tal's enthusiastic partner working with Imagine Learning
in the poorest parts of NYC
CHARITY, a terrific charter middle school blended learning specialist and teacher
and an astonishing party planner
And More important: The contributions they are all making in Church,
And with their partnerships and children within their own families

Brag, brag, brag, but it's actually another form of Thanks-Giving!
And it feels good, so do it!
Love, from the Eyrealm

If you would like to receive the Eyres' annual Thanksgiving card each year, and other updates on gratitude, simply send your email address to

EyresThanksgiving@Familius.com

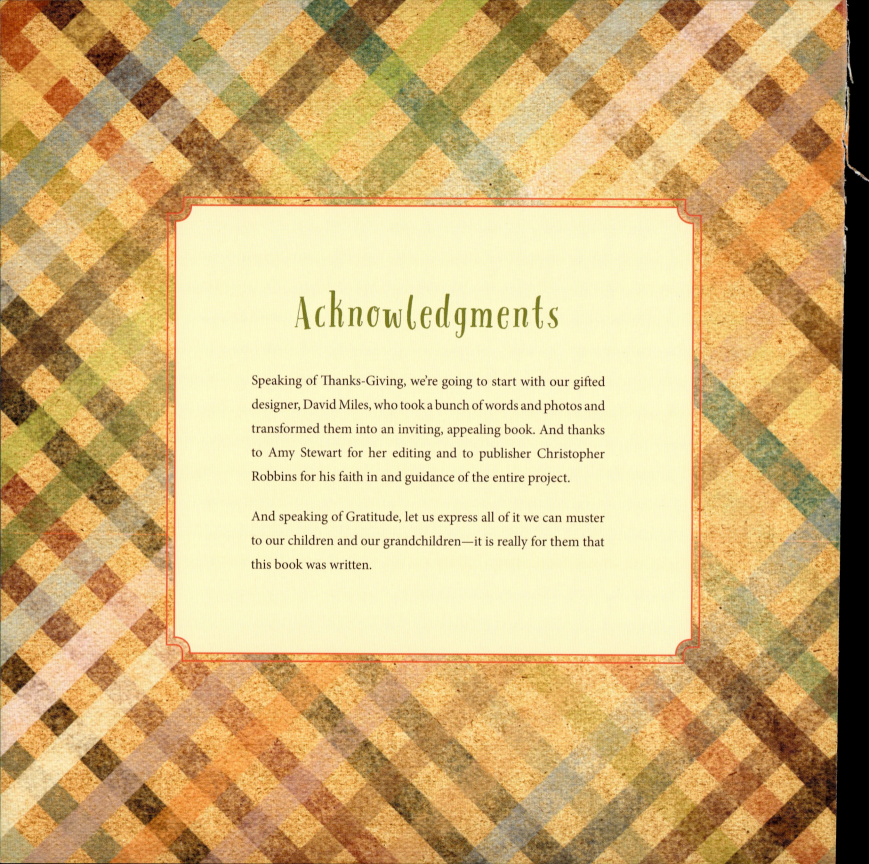

Acknowledgments

Speaking of Thanks-Giving, we're going to start with our gifted designer, David Miles, who took a bunch of words and photos and transformed them into an inviting, appealing book. And thanks to Amy Stewart for her editing and to publisher Christopher Robbins for his faith in and guidance of the entire project.

And speaking of Gratitude, let us express all of it we can muster to our children and our grandchildren—it is really for them that this book was written.

About the Authors

LINDA AND RICHARD EYRE live in Park City, Utah, except when they are traveling to keep up with their kids, visit their grandchildren, or lecture somewhere in the world on family, parenting, and life balance. They are now trying to shift their focus from prose to poetry, from the summer to the autumn of life, and from accomplishing things to being receivers and partakers of the good and the free.

About the Photographers

SHAWNI EYRE POTHIER is a mom, a sought-after speaker and professional photographer, and a blogger extraordinaire. She was named the National Young Mother of the Year in 2012 by the American Mothers Association. Her photography is widely acclaimed, and her mommy blog, 71 Toes, receives over one million visits every month. She lives with her entrepreneur-and-China-consultant husband, Dave, and their five children in Gilbert, Arizona.

R. JOSHUA EYRE is a third-grade teacher in Gilbert, Arizona, who is recognized for both the creativity and individual devotion of his teaching. A decade ago, he moved from a lucrative building and development career to his real love of teaching and has never looked back. His second career, photography, has taken him to the far corners of the earth, where he loves photographing nature and indigenous people.

SAYDRIA EYRE SHUMWAY is the mother of four, a Columbia University–trained social worker, and a portrait and family photographer. She gave up a promising singing and acting career to pursue her passions of family, art, and helping the poor. With degrees from Wellesley College and Columbia, she lives with her husband, Jeff, a social-impact bond financier, and their four children in the Boston area.

ELIJAH EYRE and his wife, Julie, live on the Upper West Side of Manhattan, where they have recently started their family with their daughter, Zara. Julie is a pediatric nurse while Eli manages the New York City area for Imagine Learning—a company devoted to teaching English as a second language to immigrant public school kids—and practices his photographic skills on architecture and nature shots.

EVA KOLEVA TIMOTHY came from her home in Bulgaria to live with the Eyre family when she was a teenager. She honed her photographic gift while studying at Oxford University in England and has exhibited and won recognition for her unique photos in Europe as well as America. Eva and her musician-businessman husband, Adam, live in the artists' community of Newburyport, Massachussetts, with their three home-schooled children.

ELLE POTHIER is a high school junior who gets As, plays varsity tennis, drives boys to distraction, and challenges her mom for the position of best photographer in the family.

About Familius

Welcome to a place where mothers are celebrated, not compared. Where heart is at the center of our families, and family at the center of our homes. Where boo boos are still kissed, cake beaters are still licked, and mistakes are still okay. Welcome to a place where books—and family—are beautiful. Familius: a book publisher dedicated to helping families be happy.

Visit Our Website: www.familius.com

Our website is a different kind of place. Get inspired, read articles, discover books, watch videos, connect with our family experts, download books and apps and audiobooks, and along the way, discover how values and happy family life go together.

Join Our Family

There are lots of ways to connect with us! Subscribe to our newsletters at www.familius.com to receive uplifting daily inspiration, essays from our Pater Familius, a free ebook every month, and the first word on special discounts and Familius news.

Become an Expert

Familius authors and other established writers interested in helping families be happy are invited to join our family and contribute online content. If you have something important to say on the family, join our expert community by applying at:

www.familius.com/apply-to-become-a-familius-expert

Get Bulk Discounts

If you feel a few friends and family might benefit from what you've read, let us know and we'll be happy to provide you with quantity discounts. Simply email us at specialorders@familius.com.

Website: www.familius.com
Facebook: www.facebook.com/paterfamilius
Twitter: @familiustalk, @paterfamilius1
Pinterest: www.pinterest.com/familius

FAMILIUS

THE MOST IMPORTANT WORK YOU EVER DO WILL BE WITHIN THE WALLS OF YOUR OWN HOME.